CCP
Certification Study Guide

Second Edition

Companion Workbook to *Skills & Knowledge of Cost Engineering,* 6th Edition

Dr. Makarand Hastak, PE CCP, Editor

2016

CCP Certification Study Guide
Second Edition
Copyright © 2006-2016
by
AACE® International
1265 Suncrest Towne Centre Drive, Morgantown, WV 26505-1876, USA
Phone: +1.304.2968444 | Fax: +1.304.2915728 | E-mail: education@aacei.org | Web:
www.aacei.org

A Publication of

CCP Certification Study Guide

Second Edition

Dr. Makarand Hastak, PE CCP, Editor

A continuing project of the AACE International Education Board

AACE International Publications Staff:
Formatting and Layout: Marvin Gelhausen, Managing Editor
Cover Design: Noah Kinderknecht, Art Director
Cassandra LoPiccolo, Social Media and Publications Intern

Editorial Team:

Editor:
Dr. Makarand Hastak, PE CCP

Associate Editors:
Chris A. Boyd, CCP CEP
Mark T. Chen, PE CCP FAACE AACE Hon. Life
Dr. John O. Evans III, PSP
Clive D. Francis, CCP FAACE AACE Hon. Life
Peter W. Griesmyer, FAACE
Sean T. Regan, CCP CEP FAACE
Rohit Singh, PE CCP
James G. Zack, Jr., CFCC FAACE AACE Hon. Life

Table of Contents

PREFACE

The *Certified Cost Professional (CCP) Certification Study Guide*, 2nd Edition (CSG-2) is a companion workbook to the *Skills and Knowledge of Cost Engineering*, 6th Edition (S&K-6). The design and layout of this study guide is intended to assist readers in testing their knowledge of cost engineering by offering practice problems and questions related to the subject matter addressed in S&K-6. First published in 1996 as the *CCC/CCE Certification Study Guide*, the *CCP Certification Study Guide* has gone through several revisions and changes. In 2013 the name of the study guide was changed to the *CCP Certification Study Guide* to reflect the consolidation of CCC/CCE credentials by AACE International. For the latest information on all of the AACE certifications, visit the AACE International website at: www.aacei.org

How to Use this Book

The chapters and topics presented in this publication correspond to specific chapters in the *Skills and Knowledge of Cost Engineering* (S&K-6). The reader should use this publication in conjunction with S&K-6. Together, these publications provide readers with the knowledge base expected of a cost-engineering professional as outlined in Recommended Practice 11R-88, *Required Skills and Knowledge of Cost Engineering* and the *TCM Framework*, 2nd Edition. This publication has two specific objectives:

1. To provide a summary of specific knowledge areas and the associated key terms that a cost engineering professional should comprehend, at a minimum, when preparing for the Certified Cost Professional (CCP) certification exam.
2. To provide sample problems and questions for each topic area, as well as the associated answers, to exercise the reader's understanding of the concepts and skills presented in S&K-6.

The S&K-6 and CCP CSG-2 are companion publications which serve as reference texts for individuals preparing for the Certified Cost Professional (CCP) and other AACE International certification examinations. To further assist in preparation, the reader should visit the AACE International website at www.aacei.org for updates to the CCP certification as well as Recommended Practice 10S-90, *Cost Engineering Terminology*.

Readers should begin their examination preparation by first studying the material presented in S&K-6 and then working out the sample problems and questions in the CCP CSG-2. The summary and key terms found in each chapter offer a checklist of the comprehensive knowledge needed to fully prepare for the examination. Readers may have to go back and forth between the two publications to gain a full understanding of the subject matter as they attempt the exercise problems and questions. Please note that the actual certification examination questions are likely to address skills and knowledge from multiple chapters; therefore, a thorough understanding of the material is vitally important. In addition, the CCP CSG-2 includes several key appendices such as: (1) sample exam questions, (2) values of the standard normal distribution, and (3) the discrete compound interest tables.

Acknowledgements

This work is an undertaking of the AACE Education Board. A work of this magnitude and quality cannot be completed without dedicated contributions from (i) the Education Board champions/associate editors who identified subject matter experts and diligently followed up with them to write and/or revise the chapter summaries and the related questions, (ii) all the authors for their contribution to this publication, (iii) the reviewers who methodically evaluated each chapter for accuracy and depth of questions covered, as well as, (iv) my graduate students - Sayanti

Mukhopadhyay and Saumyang Patel and all the AACE staff who worked with me and contributed countless hours in making this project successful. My special thanks are due to Mark Chen and John Hines for their support and dedication in getting this project completed. Mark Chen's management and diplomatic skills were particularly helpful in keeping the entire team on track toward the successful completion of this publication. It has been an honor to have worked with all these dedicated individuals and I sincerely appreciate their efforts and support throughout this project.

We hope you find this publication to be of value. The Education Board welcomes any comments and suggestions you might have in improving the *Certification Study Guide* (CSG-2) as well as the *Skills and Knowledge of Cost Engineering* (S&K-6).

Prof. Makarand Hastak, Ph.D., PE, CCP
Purdue University
October 2015

CONTRIBUTORS

Editor
Dr. Makarand Hastak, PE CCP

Cost Elements
Franklin D. Postula, PE CCP FAACE
AACE Hon. Life (Deceased)
Chris A. Boyd, CCP CEP

Pricing and Costing
Rohit Singh, P. Eng. CCP

Materials
Neil D. Opfer, CCP CEP PSP FAACE

Labor
Morris E. Fleishman, PE CCP
FAACE

Engineering Role and Project Success
Neil D. Opfer, CCP CEP PSP FAACE

Machinery, Equipment, and Tools
Dr. Carl C. Chrappa

Economic Costs
Neil D. Opfer, CCP CEP PSP FAACE

Activity-Based Cost Management
Gary Cokins

Cost Estimating
Larry R. Dysert, CCP DRMP FAACE
AACE Hon. Life

Process Product Manufacturing
Dr. Kenneth K. Humphreys, PE
CCP FAACE

Discrete Part Manufacturing
Dr. Robert C. Creese, PE CCP

Project Planning
James A. Bent, CCP (Deceased)
Jennifer Bates, CCP FAACE AACE
Hon. Life
Peter W. Griesmyer, FAACE

Scheduling
Anthony J. Werderitsch, PE CCP
CFCC FAACE AACE Hon. Life

Earned Value Overview
Sean T. Regan, CCP CEP FAACE

Performance and Productivity Management
Dr. James M. Neil, PE CCP AACE
Hon. Life (Deceased)
Rohit Singh, P. Eng. CCP

Project Management Fundamentals
James A. Bent, CCP (Deceased)
Madhu P. Pillai, CCP
Sean T. Regan, CCP CEP FAACE
Neil D. Opfer, CCP CEP PSP FAACE

Project Organization Structure
James A. Bent, CCP (Deceased)
Madhu P. Pillai, CCP
Sean T. Regan, CCP CEP FAACE

Project Communications
Joseph A. Lukas, PE CCP

Project Labor Cost Control
Dr. Joseph J. Orczyk, PE CCP
Sean T. Regan, CCP CEP FAACE

Leadership and Management of Project People
Dr. Ginger Levin
Madhu P. Pillai, CCP

Quality Management
Gary Cokins

Value Engineering
Neil D. Opfer, CCP CEP PSP FAACE

Contracting for Capital Projects
James G. Zack, Jr., CFCC FAACE
AACE Hon. Life

Strategic Asset Management
John K. Hollmann, PE CCP CEP
DRMP FAACE AACE Hon. Life

Change Management Practical Guide
Sean T. Regan, CCP CEP FAACE

Overview of Construction Claims and Disputes
John C. Livengood, Esq., AIA CCP
CFCC PSP FAACE
James G. Zack, Jr., CFCC FAACE
AACE Hon. Life

Financial and Cash Flow Analysis
Dr. Scott J. Amos, PE

Practical Corporate Investment Decision-Making Guide
J. D. (Jim) Whiteside, II, PE FAACE

Statistics and Probability
Dr. Elizabeth Y. Chen
Mark T. Chen, PE CCP FAACE
AACE Hon. Life

Optimization
Dr. Robert C. Creese, PE CCP

Risk Management Fundamentals
Allen C. Hamilton, CCP

Risk Management Practical Guide
Allen C. Hamilton, CCP

Total Cost Management Overview
Larry R. Dysert, CCP DRMP FAACE
AACE Hon. Life

The International System of Units (SI)
Kurt G. R. Heinze, P. Eng. CCP
FAACE AACE Hon. Life

AACE Publications Staff
Marvin Gelhausen
Noah Kinderknecht

Purdue Graduate Students
Sayanti Mukhopadhyay
Saumyang Patel

SECTION 1 – COST

Chapter 1 – Cost Elements

Frank D. Postula, PE CCP FAACE AACE Hon. Life

Introduction/Learning Objectives

Cost is one of the three fundamental attributes associated with performing an activity or the acquisition of an asset. These are: price (cost), features (performance), and availability (schedule). The key learning objectives are:

- Understand what makes up cost – i.e., the basic resources (material, labor, etc.) that are needed to perform an activity or create an asset.
- Understand the distinction between cost elements that are directly applied to an asset and those that are indirectly applied.
- Relate the cost elements to the life cycle of the asset: acquisition, use and disposal.
- Use the understanding of cost elements to further understand how cost is measured, applied, and recorded to arrive at the total activity and/or asset cost.
- Apply the knowledge gained to solve problems related to cost element source and definition.

Terms to Know

- Activity
- Asset
- Cost
- Cost categories
- Cost elements
- Cost objectives
- Direct costs
- Fixed costs
- Indirect costs
- Project
- Resources
- Variable costs
- Work breakdown structure (WBS)

Key Points for Review

❖ **Concepts**
  - Cost engineering is the application of scientific principles and techniques.
  - What are the key activities that generate cost when they are performed or that define plans and processes that cause (or influence) cost to be generated in other activities and/or assets?
  - What are the elements that make up cost?
  - How are these cost elements categorized and how do they relate to one another?
  - Why is it important to collect and account for costs as they relate to specific activities and assets?

o How to apply these cost elements and categories to the insight for managing activities and assets?

❖ **Cost Definition**
  o Cost is the value of an activity or asset.
  o Resources used are categorized as material, labor, and "other."
  o The value of the asset may also include the cost elements of scrap material or manufacturing spares, construction form-work and expendable safety items, as well as the cost of transporting the material to the work site.

❖ **Material**
  o Material is the physical composition of the asset. However, the value of the asset may also include the cost elements of scrap material or manufacturing spares, construction form work and expendable safety items, and the cost of transporting the material to the work site.

❖ **Labor**
  o Labor as the value of the work needed to complete the activity or asset.

❖ **Other**
  o The "other" cost category is resources that are needed to support the activity and/or asset.

❖ **Cost Category and Value of Asset**
  o Another important aspect of cost relates to whether one is the producer or consumer of an activity or asset.
  o The value of an asset or activity may also be related to intangible costs.

Category	Cost Element Examples
Material	Pen, desk, lumber, etc.
Labor	Draw plans, order materials, receive materials, installation, etc.
Other	Permit fees, gas, truck, etc.

❖ **Cost Structure**
  o It is important to further structure the cost elements within the material, labor, and other resource categories in order to understand how they influence the total cost of the activity or asset and to get a better understanding of how they can be controlled.

❖ **Grouping**
The cost elements can be grouped into direct costs, indirect costs, fixed costs, and variable costs.

  o **Direct costs** are those resources that are expended solely to complete the activity or an asset. In other words, any cost that is specifically identified with a particular final cost objective, but not necessarily limited to items that are incorporated in the end product as material or labor is considered direct cost.
  o **Indirect costs** are those resources that need to be expended to support the activity or asset, but are also associated with other activities and assets. In other words, any cost not directly

identified with a single final cost objective, but identified with two or more final cost objectives. Indirect costs may also be referred to as "overhead costs" or "burden costs." Indirect costs are general administrative activities associated with operating the business, costs for providing and maintaining field equipment or a manufacturing facility, and expenses for utilities, taxes, legal services, etc.

- o **Fixed costs** are those cost elements that must be provided independent of the volume of work activity or asset production that they support. These can be either direct or indirect costs.
- o **Variable costs** are those cost elements that must be provided and are dependent on the volume of work activity or asset production that they support. Again, these can be either direct or indirect costs.
- o Grouping examples can be found in Chapter 1, *Skills and Knowledge of Cost Engineering*, 6th Edition, Tables 1.2 and 1.4.

❖ **Cost Accounting Definition:**
- o Cost accounting is defined as the historical reporting of disbursements, costs and expenditures on a project.
- o Recording of cost information is nothing more than the mechanical gathering of data in a routine manner.
- o Become familiar with the code of accounts structure.
- o Activity based costing assigns resources to activities.
- o Work breakdown structure (WBS) can be used with code of accounts. Be familiar with the structure.

❖ **Cost Management**
The four common methods for providing cost information as they apply to cost management are as follows:

- o **Cost Estimating**: This is the prediction of the quantity and cost of resources needed to accomplish an activity or create an asset.
- o **Cost Trending**: Cost trends are established from historical cost accounting information. Cost management questions may focus on how expenditures are trending relative to physical accomplishments.
- o **Cost Forecasting**: Forecasts are much like estimates. Whereas an estimate is always for future activities and assets, forecasts are prediction of the cost at completion for cost elements that are in progress.
- o **Life-Cycle Costing**: Life-cycle costs (LCC) are associated with an asset and extend the cost management information beyond the acquisition (creation) of the asset to the use and disposal of the asset.

Check on Learning

1. _____ are those cost elements that must be provided and dependent on the volume of work activity or asset production that they support.

    A. Direct Costs
    B. Indirect Costs
    C. Fixed Costs
    D. Variable Costs

2. _____ is a method of cost element classification where resources are assigned to activities that are required to accomplish a cost objective.

    A. Code of Accounts
    B. Summary Level Accounts
    C. Activity Based Costing
    D. Work Breakdown Structure

3. _____ are those cost elements that must be provided independent of the volume of work activity or asset production that they support.

    A. Direct Costs
    B. Indirect Costs
    C. Fixed Costs
    D. Variable Costs

4. _____ are those resources that are expended solely to complete the activity or asset.

    A. Direct Costs
    B. Indirect Costs
    C. Fixed Costs
    D. Variable Costs

5. _____ are associated with an asset and extend the cost management information beyond the acquisition (creation) of the asset to the use and disposal of the asset.

    A. Life-Cycle Costs (LCC)
    B. Indirect Costs
    C. Fixed Costs
    D. Variable Costs

6. _____ are those cost elements that must be provided and difficult to appropriate as a direct cost on specific assets that they support.

    A. Direct Costs
    B. Indirect Costs
    C. Fixed Costs
    D. Variable Costs

7. The work breakdown structure (WBS) can be an effective aid for which type of communications?

    A. Team
    B. Company
    C. Customer
    D. All of the above

8. Which of the following is a key reason to use a work breakdown structure (WBS)?

    A. Organize the work
    B. Prevent work from slipping through the cracks
    C. Provide a basis for estimating the project
    D. All of the above

9. Which of the following is not an example of a variable?

    A. Size
    B. Shape
    C. Stamping tool
    D. Weight

10. Procurement planning involves:

    A. A make or buy decision
    B. Answering supplier's questions
    C. Creating the contract
    D. Creating the RFP

Solutions

1.   D   Variable Costs
   > Refer to Chapter 1, "Cost Structuring" topic

2.   C   Activity Based Costing
   > Refer to Chapter 1, "Cost Structuring" topic

3.   C   Fixed Cost
   > Refer to Chapter 1, "Cost Structuring" topic

4.   A   Direct Cost
   > Refer to Chapter 1, "Cost Structuring" topic

5.   A   Life-Cycle Costs (LCC)
   > Refer to Chapter 1, "Cost Management" topic

6.   B   Indirect Cost
   > Refer to Chapter 1, "Cost Structuring" topic

7.   D   All of the above
   > Refer to Chapter 1, "Cost Structuring" topic

8.   D   All the above
   > Refer to Chapter 1, "Cost Structuring" topic

9.   C   Stamping tool
   > Refer to Chapter 1, "Cost Structuring" topic

10.   A   A make or buy decision
    > Refer to Chapter 1, "Cost Management" topic

Chapter 2 – Pricing and Costing

Rohit (Roy) Singh, P.Eng. M.Ed., CCP

Introduction/Learning Objectives

This chapter highlights the difference between pricing and costing. It is very important to distinguish between the terms "price" and "cost." There is a very fine difference between them, which is why people often tend to use them interchangeably. This chapter discusses the concepts of pricing and costing of a project, illustrates the differences and helps the reader to identify the inputs, transforming mechanisms and outputs related to the costing and pricing process. The key learning objectives are:

- Differentiate between costing and pricing.
- Identify the inputs, transforming mechanisms and outputs related to the cost and pricing process.
- Understand the budgeting process.
- Calculate financial ratios related to the costing and pricing of projects.
- Understand the reasoning behind the costing and pricing process outputs.

Terms to Know

- Cash flow
- Competitive advantage
- Cost
- Financial management
- Inputs
- Opportunity cost
- Outputs
- Price
- Profit
- Return on assets (ROA)
- Return on investment (ROI)
- Transforming mechanism

Key Points for Review

❖ **Costing and Pricing**
  - Costing follows scope determination and quantification and precedes pricing and budgeting.
  - Cost can be categorized into direct or indirect cost.
  - Direct costs are those that are specific and tangible to the project, and include the costs of materials, labor, equipment, etc.
  - Indirect costs are those costs not directly accountable or tangible to the project, such as business taxes, home office overhead, or transportation fleet distributed cost.
  - Pricing can be defined as the determination of the amount to be charged to the client including:
    - ✓ Direct cost

- ✓ Indirect cost
- ✓ Contingency
- ✓ Profit
  - o Seller vs buyer perspective determines price vs cost – e.g. $100,000 transaction
    - ✓ $100,000 is the price including profit from seller's perspective
    - ✓ $100,000 is the cost from the buyer's perspective
  - o Cost-Pricing Process Inputs
    - ✓ WBS/Scope
    - ✓ Historical records
    - ✓ Vendor quotations
  - o Transforming mechanism (Tools and techniques)
    - ✓ Cost and pricing strategies
    - ✓ Financial management
  - o Outputs
    - ✓ Project estimate
    - ✓ Project acquisition
    - ✓ Business decision

- ❖ **Budgeting process**
  - o Activity cost estimates
  - o Scope baseline
  - o Project schedule
  - o Contracts

- ❖ **Forecasting**
  - o Applying earned value method
  - o Using Cost Performance Index (CPI) to calculate Estimate at Complete (EAC)
  - o Early prediction of overrun when EAC is higher than Budget at Completion (BAC)

- ❖ **Financial management**
  - o Return on investment (ROI)
  - o Return on assets (ROA)
  - o Net profit margin

- ❖ **Project Acquisition and Business Decision**
  - o Review financial ratios (e.g. ROI, ROA, net profit margin) to determine the validity of acquisitions and support business decisions.

Check on Learning

1. Which of the following is not a major step in the Cost-Pricing process?

    A. Inputs
    B. Transforming mechanisms (Tools & Techniques)
    C. Outputs
    D. Bid award

2. Which item is not a major output to the Cost-Pricing process?

    A. Project Estimate
    B. Project acquisition
    C. Business decision
    D. Resource loaded CPM schedule

3. Which item is not considered a direct cost?

    A. Labor
    B. Material
    C. Site overhead
    D. Equipment

4. Historical records for costing and pricing a project does not include:

    A. Quantity take-offs
    B. Cost reports
    C. Competitor pricing
    D. Bid breakdowns

5. Inputs to the costing- pricing process do not include:

    A. Scope of work
    B. Historical records
    C. Vendor quotations
    D. Sales forecasts

6. Inputs to the budget development process include:

    A. Activity cost estimates
    B. Scope baseline
    C. Project schedule
    D. All of the above

7. Which financial management tool is best for comparing projects in the same industry?

    A. Net profit margin
    B. Return on assets
    C. Gross profit margin
    D. Break-even analysis

8. In regards to the difference between price and cost, which statement is incorrect?

    A. The vendor's price is the cost to the contractor
    B. The vendor's price plus the contractor's markup is the cost to the client
    C. The bid price to the owner is the contractor's cost
    D. The subcontractor quote is the contractor's cost

Solutions

1.   D   Bid Award
   > Refer to Chapter 2, "Cost-Pricing Process" topic & Figure 2.2

2.   D   Resource Loaded Schedule
   > Refer to Chapter 2, "Cost-Pricing Process" topic & Figure 2.2

3.   C   Site Overhead is not considered a direct cost
   > Refer to Chapter 2, Figure 2.1

4.   C   Competitor pricing
   > Refer to Chapter 2, "Historical Records" topic

5.   D   Sales Forecasts
   > Refer to Chapter 2, "Inputs" topic & Figure 2.2

6.   D   All of the above
   > Refer to Chapter 2, "Budgeting" topic

7.   B   Return on Assets
   > Refer to Chapter 2, "Financial Management" topic

8.   C   The bid price to the owner is the contractor's cost
   > Refer to Chapter 2, "Conclusion" topic

Chapter 3 – Materials

Neil D. Opfer, CCP CEP PSP FAACE

Introduction/Learning Objectives

Materials are the key resource in most of the projects and production endeavors. Materials are purchased by those using them, rather than being manufactured by the subject entity. Materials range from the simplest of raw materials to the most complex fabricated materials with a large range in between. This chapter provides a basic understanding of the use of raw and finished materials (as a resource) in projects and production/manufacturing processes. The key learning objectives are:

- Identify types of project materials
- Understand the issues involved in selecting and handling materials
- Understand the principles of materials purchasing and management, including the proper amount of stock to save money and avoid waste or production delays
- Understand possible safety hazards associated with materials and be aware of regulations governing worker and materials safety
- Understand the relationship of 'material' topics to the cost engineering processes of estimating, economic analysis, value engineering, planning, scheduling and project management

Terms to Know

- Bulk material
- Competing characteristics
- Engineered materials
- Fabricated material
- Handling, raw material
- Procurement
- Safety stock
- Surplus
- Waste

Key Points for Review

❖ **Materials Competition**
  ○ Economical and market forces often drive the selection of a particular material to use in the finished product/project.
  ○ Balancing best possible use/material type with risk, selling economics, safety and intended use is necessary.

❖ **Materials Handling Considerations**
  ○ It includes balancing of the cost and efficiency of materials handling issues.

❖ **Materials Handling Principles**

- o Material movement should be over the shortest distance possible
- o Terminal time should be in the shortest time possible
- o Eliminate manual material handling when mechanized methods are feasible
- o Avoid partial transport loads
- o Materials should be readily identifiable and retrievable

❖ **Materials Handling Decision Factors**
- o Type and characteristics of material being handled
- o Sourcing and transport considerations
- o Production system considerations
- o Facility type and throughput considerations
- o Cost considerations

❖ **Material Types and Related Information**
- o **Raw materials**: used in production or fabrication
- o **Bulk materials**: partially processed or fabricated before being incorporated into a new product or facility
- o **Fabricated materials**: bulk materials transformed into custom-fit items for a particular product or project
- o **Engineered/designed materials**: require substantial engineering, procurement and construction effort to attain final form

❖ **Production Materials Purchase and Management**
- o Key to offering competitive price
- o Proper quality of materials selected/used through specifications
- o Vendor surveillance and traceability
- o Quality assurance/control
- o Economic order quantity (EOQ):

$$EOQ = [\sqrt{2xDxP/S}]$$

where:
D = annual demand; P = purchase order costs; S = storage/carrying costs

Reorder Point (RP) = [(O x R) + I]

where:
RP = reorder point; O = order time; R = production rate; I = minimum inventory level or safety stock

- o Just-In-Time (JIT) inventory techniques
- o Individual purchase orders and systems contracts
- o Materials inspection
- o Expediting
- o Global materials decisions

❖ **Plant Materials Management**
- o Not product or project specific, but mid-stream materials used in support of the production of

products or finished work elements
- o Specialized plant materials: critical equipment parts with long lead time; supplementing parts availability
- o Plant materials benchmarking: learning from other organization's material management practices

❖ **Materials Waste Product and Hazard Issues**
- o Governmental regulations compliance and communications issues:
  - ✓ Material safety data sheets (MSDS).
  - ✓ Environmental regulations: e.g. US regulates three categories of hazardous waste handlers:
    - ▪ Generators
    - ▪ Transporters
    - ▪ Owners and operators of Treatment, Storage, and Disposal facilities
- o Material life cycle: All materials have a life cycle from "cradle to grave"
- o Waste materials and surplus management.

❖ **Future Developments**
- o The use and continued advancement in computerized techniques and 3D printing.

Check on Learning

1. Which of the following statements regarding material handling is true?

    A. Poor material handling can result in damage to raw materials or the finished product
    B. Efficient material handling can slow production operations
    C. Material handling has no significant issues
    D. Material handling in not a requirement; as inefficiencies are labor based

2. All of the following decision factors affect material handling except:

    A. Material to be handled
    B. Employee type
    C. Production system type
    D. Material handling costs

3. Which one of the following represents the four basic material categories?

    A. Rare materials, surplus materials, fabricated materials, engineered/designed materials
    B. Raw materials, bulk materials, fabricated materials, engineered/designed materials
    C. Raw materials, bulk materials, fabricated materials, long lead materials
    D. Raw materials, pre-packed materials, fabricated materials, engineered/designed materials

4. Which one of the following represents the three general areas affecting the production materials purchased and management?

    A. Materials specifications, material vendor surveillance and traceability, materials quantity
    B. Materials quality, material vendor surveillance and traceability, materials cost
    C. Materials quality, material vendor volume and production, materials quantity
    D. Materials quality, material vendor surveillance and traceability, materials quantity

5. Which of the following is not used to calculate Economic Order Quantity?

    A. Annual demand
    B. Production rate
    C. Purchase order costs
    D. Storage/carrying costs

6. Which of the following is not used to calculate the Reorder Point?

    A. Order time
    B. Sales
    C. Production rate
    D. Safety stock

7. US Resource Conservation and Recovery Act (RCRA) does not regulate the following category:

   A. Pipelines
   B. Generators
   C. Transporters
   D. Owners and operators of TSD facilities

8. The Globally Harmonized System (GHS) of Classification and Labeling of Chemicals, is a system for standardizing and harmonizing the classification and labeling of chemicals. It addresses the following:

   A. Defining health, physical, and environmental hazards of chemicals;
   B. Creating classification processes that use available data on chemicals for comparison with the defined hazard criteria; and,
   C. Communicating hazard information, as well as protective measures, on labels and Material Safety Data Sheets (MSDS)
   D. All of the above

9. Which statement applies to Just-in-Time techniques for materials procurement?

   A. Remove safety stocks
   B. Cause fast tracking
   C. Cost more than they save
   D. Is not actually a procurement strategy

Solutions

1.   A   Poor Material handling can result in damage to raw materials or the finished product
           Refer to Chapter 3, "Material Handling Decision Factors" topic

2.   B   Employee type
           Refer to Chapter 3, "Material Handling Decision Factors" topic

3.   B   Raw materials, bulk materials, fabricated materials, engineered/design materials.
           Refer to Chapter 3, "Types of Material and Related Information" topic

4.   D   Materials quality, material vendor surveillance and traceability, materials quantity.
           Refer to Chapter 3, "Production Materials Purchase and Management" topic

5.   B   Production rate
           Refer to Chapter 3, "Economic Order Quantity" topic

6.   B   Sales
           Refer to Chapter 3, "Economic Order Quantity" topic

7.   A   Pipelines
           Refer to Chapter 3, "Environmental regulations" topic

8.   D   All of the above
           Refer to Chapter 3, "Safety Data Sheets and Hazard Communication" topic

9.   A   Remove Safety Stocks
           Refer to Chapter 3, "Just-In-Time Inventory Techniques" topic

Chapter 4 – Labor

Morris E. Fleishman, PE CCP FAACE

Introduction/Learning Objectives

Labor is one of the most important resources for a project. An owner, employer, or a project manager of any industry needs to have a complete understanding of how the labor force works. This chapter provides an overview of the different classifications of labor, the different types of labor wages and benefits and also indirect and overhead labor and other costs. This chapter also illustrates the methodology of determining realistic value of labor cost. The key learning objectives are:

- Identify different classifications of labor and how each contributes to the final completed project.
- Develop labor rates for estimating.
- Develop and use weighted average rates/composite crew rates.
- Include indirect and overhead labor and other costs.
- Estimate work hours for a given work scope at a given location.
- Use labor hours to monitor work progress.

Terms to Know

- Direct labor
- Indirect labor
- Labor rates
- Labor wage
- Overhead labor
- Performance monitoring

Key Points for Review

❖ **Labor classifications**
  o Direct labor
  o Indirect labor
  o Overhead labor

❖ **Basic Wage:**
  o Sources of basic wages data may include:
    ✓ Data bases from previous projects
    ✓ Labor contracts
    ✓ Unit rates supplied by contracting and engineering firms
    ✓ Local chamber of commerce data
    ✓ Government labor statistics
    ✓ Published labor data bases
    ✓ Standardized estimating publications such as Means and Aspen

❖ **Fringe Benefits**
  o Paid time off
  o Medical and life insurance benefits
  o Government mandated benefits

❖ **Engineering/Contractors Overhead and Profit**
  o Base wages including fringes
  o Worker's Compensation (if applicable)
  o Overhead
  o Profit (if applicable for time and material situations)

❖ **Fully Loaded or Billing Rate**
  o Sick time
  o Vacation
  o Holidays

❖ **Overtime Wages**
  o Premium wage paid for work in excess of regular working hours
  o Some benefits are not added to overtime hours
  o Social Security and Medicare are calculated as a percentage added to overtime rate

❖ **Weighted Average Rates/Crew Composition Rates**
  o Average of differing experience and skill levels

❖ **Methods for Estimating Indirect and Overhead Labor Cost**
  o Total staff hours applied to wage rates to compute indirect labor
  o Historical data to compute adders for indirect labor costs

❖ **Estimating Work Hours to Complete a Job**
  o Labor productivity adjustment factors
  o Learning curve (experience curve) and its effect on productivity

❖ **Performance Monitoring**
  o Earned value computations (SPI and CPI)
    ✓ SPI = BCWP (EV)/ BCWS (PV)
    ✓ CPI = BCWP (EV)/ ACWP (AC)
  o Understanding how to use graphical presentation of earned value data

❖ **Work Sampling**
  o Method to determine production or unit rates for specific work activities
  o Used in setting up a company database, or determining the relationship between work at an individual site and labor standards, which have been or may be used for estimating projects in the future
  o Comparisons can then be made against existing experience or databases to determine the most reasonable data to use as the standard
  o Used for estimating projects in the future
  o The data can be used to determine how the actual work is deviating from the standard

Check on Learning

1. In a 40-hour per week work year, how many hours would a machinist work given the following:

   - Sick leave allowed = 5 days
   - Vacation days = 10 days
   - Paid holidays = 10 days

   Assume that all sick time is used.

   - A. 2040 hours
   - B. 1960 hours
   - C. 1880 hours
   - D. 1920 hours

2. You have the following crew mix. Calculate the composite direct crew hourly wage.

XYZ Production Crew	Direct Wage
1 Foreman	$25.00 per/hr.
2 Operators	$18.00 per/hr.
2 Helpers	$12.00 per/hr.
1 Mechanic	$15.00 per/hr.

   - A. $11.67
   - B. $25.00
   - C. $16.67
   - D. $20.00

3. The following personnel are assigned to a construction project. Classify them into indirect and overhead personnel and calculate the per hour cost added per direct work hour for each classification. The total direct work-hours are 10,000 for the month.

	No.	Hrs./month	Wages/hr.
Payroll Personnel	2	172	$35
Procurement	2	10	$40
Plant Cost and Scheduling	3	172	$45
Human Resources	2	25	$45
Corporate Computer Support	5	50	$55
Construction Management	3	172	$60

   - A. Indirects = $1.68, Overheads = $6.62
   - B. Indirects = $6.62, Overheads = $1.68
   - C. Indirects = $3.53, Overheads = $4.78
   - D. Indirects = $1.60, Overheads = $6.70

4. Given the standard labor cost for 100 LF of footing 8 inches by 12 inches = $125.00, if the jobsite conditions are:

   • Jobsite conditions: average
   • Worker Skill: poor
   • Temperature: 80 degrees
   • Work week: 50 hours

   What is the adjusted unit rate given the factors below?

Jobsite conditions	Good	+4%
	Average	+7%
	Poor	+12%
Worker skill level	High	+3.5%
	Average	+8%
	Poor	+15.5%
Temperature	Below 40°F or above 85°F, add 1 percent per degree of variance	
Work weeks in excess of 40 hours	40 – 48 hours	+7.5%
	49 – 50 hours	+13.5%
	51 – 54 hours	+18%
	55 – 59 hours	+23%

   A. $161.25
   B. $170.00
   C. $153.13
   D. $165.00

5. You are given the following information for a five-day work activity:

Description	Day 1	Day 2	Day 3	Day 4	Day 5	CPI	SPI
Cumulative hours (plan)	60	85	136	175	215		
Actual hours expended	48	72	144				
Cumulative hours earned							
Cumulative earned percentages	15%	28%	57%				

   Calculate the cumulative hours earned and determine the CPI and the SPI.

   A. CPI = 0.90, SPI = 0.85
   B. CPI = 0.54, SPI = 0.57
   C. CPI = 0.85, SPI = 0.90
   D. CPI = 1.18, SPI = 1.11

6. You are 10 weeks into a project and the following information is in your weekly project status report:

- CPI = 1.02
- SPI = 0.98

These indicators mean:

   A. Project is ahead of schedule and over budget
   B. Project is behind schedule and under budget
   C. Project is behind schedule and over budget
   D. Project is ahead of schedule and under budget

7. Which of the following are U.S. and State government mandated labor benefits?

   A. Medicare, Social Security, & State Unemployment
   B. State Unemployment, 401k, & Vacation
   C. Medicare, Social Security, & State Retirement Fund
   D. Medicare, Social Security, & Travel, Per Diem, & Lodging

8. One of the most important items affecting the learning curve is the productivity improvement that results from a crew performing _____ type operations.

   A. Non-repetitive
   B. Repetitive
   C. Skill of the Craft
   D. Machining

9. One common way to compute Estimate at Completion (EAC) is to take the Budget at Completion (BAC) and:

   A. Divide by SPI
   B. Multiply by SPI
   C. Multiply by CPI
   D. Divide by CPI

Solutions

1.   C

52 weeks x 5 days per week x 8 hours per day	= 2,080 hours
Less: Sick time @ 5 days x 8 hours	= -40 hours
Vacation @ 10 days x 8 hours	= -80 hours
Holidays @ 10 days x 8 hours	= -80 hours
S/T	= -200 hours

Answer = 1,880 hours

      Refer to Chapter 4, "Fringe Benefits" topic

2.   C

1 x $25.00	= $25.00
2 x $18.00	= $36.00
2 x $12.00	= $24.00
1 x $15.00	= $15.00
6	$100.00

Composite crew hourly wage = $100/6 = $16.67

      Refer to Chapter 4, "Developing Labor Rates" topic

3.   B

Indirects	No.	Hrs./Mth.	Wages/Hr.	Total	
Construction Management	3	172	$60	3x172x60	= $30,960
Plant Cost and Scheduling	3	172	$45	3x172x45	= $23,220
Payroll Personnel	3	172	$35	2x172x35	= $12,040
					= $66,220

Indirect Allocation = $66,220/10,000 direct work hours = $6.62 per work hour

Overhead	No.	Hrs./Mth.	Wages/Hr.	Total	
Procurement	2	10	$40	2x10x40	= $800
Human Resources	2	25	$45	2x25x45	= $2,250
Corp. Computer Support	5	50	$55	2x50x55	= $13,750
					= $16,800

Overhead Allocation = $16,800/10,000 direct work hours = $1.68 per work hour

      Refer to Chapter 4, "Indirect and Overhead Labor" topic

4.   B

Adders

Jobsite conditions	Average	+7%
Worker skill	Poor	+15.5%
Temperature	80°F	+0%
Work week	50 hours	+13.5%
Total adders		+36%

Unit Rate = $125.00 x 1.36 = $170.00

      Refer to Chapter 4, "Developing Labor Rates" topic

5. C

        Day 1 earned   = .15 x 215   = 32.25
        Day 2 earned   = .28 x 215   = 60.20
        Day 3 earned   = .57 x 215   = 122.55
        CPI = earned/expended = 122.5/144   = 0.85
        SPI = earned/planned   = 122.5/136   = 0.90
                Refer to Chapter 4, "Performance Monitoring" topic

6. B   Project is behind schedule and under budget.
                Refer to Chapter 4, "Performance Monitoring" topic

7. A   Medicare, Social Security, & State Unemployment.
                Refer to Chapter 4, "Fringe Benefits" topic

8. B   Repetitive
                Refer to Chapter 4, "Learning curve" Topic

9. D   Divide by CPI
                Refer to Chapter 4, "Performance Monitoring" topic

Chapter 5 – Engineering Role and Project Success

Neil D. Opfer, CCP CEP PSP FAACE

Introduction/Learning Objectives

Provide a basic understanding of the systems and their associated cost and schedule issues that lead to efficient and effective engineering efforts. The key learning objectives are:

- Identify engineering issues involved in product, project, and process development, including research, the use of CAD/CAE/CAM, product liability, patents, trade secrets, and developing prototypes.
- Understand product and process design and production issues, including process selection, standardization, manufacturability, constructability, and "make" or "buy" issues.
- Identify production health and safety issues.
- Identify issues involved in planning facility layout.
- Design assembly and flow process charts.
- Understand other engineering production/construction concepts, such as reengineering, and relate engineering decisions on product selection to their impact on process selection.

Terms to Know

- Building Information Modeling (BIM)
- Computer aided design (CAD)
- Computer aided engineering (CAE)
- Computer aided manufacturing (CAM)
- Constructability
- Maintainability
- Manufacturability
- Patent
- Product design
- Prototype
- Reengineering
- Robot
- Standardization
- System design
- Variance analysis

Key Points for Review

❖ **Product, Project and Process Development**
  o Pure and applied research
  o Product, project, and process life cycles
  o Computer aided design/engineering—CAD/CAE
  o Computer aided manufacturing

- Prototypes
- Patents and trade secrets
- Product liability

❖ **Product, Project and Process Design**
- Standardization
- Process selection
  - ✓ Continuous production
  - ✓ Discrete production
- Manufacturability
- Constructability
- Maintainability
- Make or buy decisions
  - ✓ Making best decisions to enhance overall quality at lower cost
- Total cost of ownership considerations

❖ **Engineering Production/Construction**
- Production health and safety
- Facility layout
- Assembly and flow process charts
- Quantitative analysis in facility layout
- Reengineering

Check on Learning

1. Research that attempts to develop a usable product or new feature to an existing product is:

   A. Pure research
   B. Applied research
   C. Market research
   D. Competitive research

2. Since June 1995 in the US and generally in all industrialized countries, a patent's duration is _____?

   A. 20 years
   B. 15 years
   C. 17 years
   D. 10 years

3. Which of the following is not an advantage of standardization in manufacturing?

   A. Less investment in spare parts
   B. Shorter time to market
   C. Product flaws will be spread over a wide variety of products
   D. Fewer equipment components resulting in faster repairs

4. Which of the following is not a type of continuous production?

   A. Petro-chemical plant
   B. Machine shop
   C. Power plant
   D. Automotive manufacturer

5. Which of the following is not a type of discrete production?

   A. Concrete pre-cast plant
   B. Structural steel fabricator
   C. Manufacturers with assembly-line methods
   D. Manufacturers of custom products

6. Continuous production method systems are less expensive in the long run because _____?

   A. High demand equals lower costs
   B. Machinery is cheaper than labor
   C. Cost of equipment is amortized over many units of production
   D. Both A and C

7. Slight changes in design that do not affect the product, but instead promote ease of assembly of the product, are referred to as _____?

   A. Constructability
   B. Process selection
   C. Manufacturability
   D. Continuous production

8. Which of the following statements is false in regards to reengineering?

   A. Radical redesign of business process
   B. Focuses on the optimization of the total organization
   C. Focuses on the sub-optimization of individuals departments
   D. The objective is to achieve dramatic improvements in critical contemporary measures

9. Which approach can reduce field labor content by allowing work to off site in a controlled environment?

   A. Constructability
   B. Process selection
   C. Manufacturability
   D. Continuous production

Solutions

1.   B   Applied research
    > Refer to Chapter 5, "Pure and Applied Research" topic

2.   A   20 years
    > Refer to Chapter 5, "Patents and Trade Secrets" topic

3.   C   Product flaws will be spread over a wide variety of products
    > Refer to Chapter 5, "Standardization" topic

4.   B   Machine shop
    > Refer to Chapter 5, "Process Selection" topic

5.   C   Manufactures with assembly-line methods
    > Refer to Chapter 5, "Process Selection" topic

6.   D   Both A and C
    > Refer to Chapter 5, "Process Selection" topic

7.   C   Manufacturability
    > Refer to Chapter 5, "Manufacturability" topic

8.   C   Focuses on the sub-optimization of individuals departments
    > Refer to Chapter 5, "Reengineering" topic

9.   A   Constructability
    > Refer to Chapter 5, "Constructability" topic

Chapter 6 – Machinery, Equipment, and Tools

Dr. Carl C. Chrappa

Introduction/Learning Objectives

This chapter illustrates the management of machinery, equipment, and tools related to a project and their impact on the project schedule and the costs. An overview of how to establish an equipment valuation database and identify the different categories and subcategories of the equipment value is provided. This chapter will also discuss equipment price and cost information and the current and residual values for new and used equipment. The key learning objectives are:

- Establish an equipment valuation database and identify the different equipment value categories and subcategories.
- Research equipment price and cost information.
- Understand the factors that affect current and residual values for new and used equipment.

Terms to Know

- Fair market value-in-place
- Fair market value-in-exchange
- Fair value
- Forced liquidation value
- Orderly liquidation value
- Replacement cost
- Reproduction cost
- Residual value
- Salvage value
- Scrap value

Key Points for Review

❖ **Equipment Value Categories**
  - Replacement cost new (new equipment cost)
    - ✓ Reproduction cost
    - ✓ Replacement cost
    - ✓ Fair value

  - Market value (used equipment, secondary market value). Subcategories are ranked in decreasing order of monetary value:
    - ✓ Fair market value-in-place
    - ✓ Fair market value-in-exchange
    - ✓ Orderly liquidation value
    - ✓ Forced liquidation value
    - ✓ Salvage value/part-out value
    - ✓ Scrap value

- ❖ **Equipment Condition Terms & Definitions**
  - ○ Example 1:
    - ✓ Very Good
    - ✓ Good
    - ✓ Fair
    - ✓ Poor
    - ✓ Scrap
  - ○ Example 2:
    - ✓ Excellent
    - ✓ Good
    - ✓ Average
    - ✓ Fair
    - ✓ Poor

- ❖ **Data Filing**
  - ○ By standard industry classification (SIC)
  - ○ By equipment class and type
  - ○ By industry category
  - ○ By equipment manufacturer's name

- ❖ **Residual Value Curves**
  - ○ L-shape curve
  - ○ U-shape curve
  - ○ Regulatory change curve
  - ○ High obsolescence curve
  - ○ New tax law/high inflation curve

- ❖ **Variables Affecting Residual Value**
  - ○ Initial cost
  - ○ Maintenance
  - ○ Use, wear, and tear
  - ○ Population
  - ○ Age
  - ○ Method of sale
  - ○ Economy
  - ○ Changes in technology
  - ○ Foreign exchange
  - ○ Tax laws
  - ○ Legislation/regulation
  - ○ Location of equipment

- ❖ **Residual Value Determination Methods**
  - ○ Income approach (present value of future cash flows)
  - ○ Market approach (Trade data)
- ❖ **Caution on Using Residual Curve**

- The use of the residual curve should be only for conceptual "order of magnitude" purposes, not for determining actual residual value.

❖ **Inflation Factor**
  - Use "machine-specific" instead of "industry-specific" inflation indices to improve reliability.

Check on Learning

1. When using market value method to assess equipment value, which one of the following will have the highest value?

   A. Fair market value-in-place
   B. Orderly liquidation value
   C. Fair market value-in-exchange
   D. Salvage value/part-out value

2. Cost adjustments are applied to normalize used equipment value. Which one of the following is not generally applied to add or deduct from the used equipment sales data?

   A. The location of the sales
   B. The same equipment, but with different years of manufacture
   C. Color of the equipment
   D. Condition of the equipment

3. Owner/leasing companies routinely apply an inflation factor to analyze residual value. Which one of the following inflation factor generally yields the highest reliability?

   A. Consumer price index (CPI)
   B. Industry-specific indices
   C. Machine-specific indices
   D. ENR equipment cost indices

4. Equipment value category-Replacement Cost New has three subcategories, what are the three subcategories?

   A. Reproduction cost, replacement cost, and fair value
   B. Replacement cost, fair value, and depreciation
   C. Fair value, reproduction cost, and depreciation
   D. Depreciation, replacement cost, and salvage value

5. The "normal" residual value curve of long-lived equipment usually follows an L-shaped curve. The high-tech equipment, such as a computer, exhibits what type of curve shape?

   A. Normal
   B. Regulation change
   C. High obsolescence
   D. High inflation

6. Residual analysis formats differ from company to company, but should contain the same basic elements. Of the two more popular formats used in the industry, which item below is not an element of either format type?

    A. Manufacturer
    B. Equipment description
    C. Life expectancy
    D. Equipment serial number

7. Generally speaking, there are 12 items that should be considered in estimating residual values; which list best describes those items?

    A. Initial cost, maintenance, location of equipment, and use, wear and tear
    B. Population, age, legislation and regulation, and economy
    C. Changes in technology, foreign exchange, tax laws, and method of sales
    D. All of the above

8. From a practical standpoint in determining residual values, the _____ is oftentimes believed to be the most accurate estimating methodology, because of its reliance on sales and trade data.

    A. Market approach
    B. Cost approach
    C. Income approach
    D. Vendor inquiry approach

9. The two major categories of equipment values that are used to establish an equipment valuation database are?

    A. Replacement cost new
    B. Market value
    C. Salvage value
    D. Both A and B

10. Based on available information during a 1980's study, it was found that guarantee companies annually experienced losses (on their guarantees) in the area of only ___ percent of the total values guaranteed.

    A. 2.5
    B. 1.5
    C. 1.0
    D. 2.0

Solutions

1.   A   Fair market value-in-place yields the highest value
   Refer to Chapter 6, "Equipment Value Categories" topic

2.   C   The color of equipment is generally not considered
   Refer to Chapter 6, "Trade Data/Cost Adjustments" topic

3.   C   The machine-specific indices tailor to each type of equipment and have the highest reliability
   Refer to Chapter 6, "Calculating Residual Values" topic

4.   A   Reproduction Cost, Replacement Cost, and Fair Value
   Refer to Chapter 6, "Equipment Value Categories" topic

5.   C   High Obsolescence - The high-tech equipment has a short life and follows the high obsolescence type curve shape
   Refer to Chapter 6, "Residual Value Curves" topic

6.   D   Equipment Serial Number
   Refer to Chapter 6, "Residual Valuation Formats" topic

7.   D   All the above
   Refer to Chapter 6, "Variables That Affect Residual Value" topic

8.   A   Market Approach
   Refer to Chapter 6, "Determining Residual Value Methodology" topic

9.   D   Both A and B
   Refer to Chapter 6, "Conclusion" topic

10.   B   1.5
   Refer to Chapter 6, "Calculating Residual Values" topic

Chapter 7 – Economic Cost

Neil D. Opfer, CCP CEP PSP FAACE

Introduction/Learning Objectives

Facing the heightened global competition, cost professionals need to sharpen their knowledge and skills of economic costs. Making the right decision to pursue a project, product or service requires a sound understanding of the time value of money, tax impact, depreciation, and economic analysis techniques. The key learning objectives are:

- Evaluate, on an economic analysis basis, the differences between two or more alternative courses of action.
- Understand such concepts and techniques as depreciation methods, net present value, annual cash flow analysis, rate-of-return, benefit-cost analysis, and payback periods.

Terms to Know

- Benefit-cost ratio
- Depletion
- Depreciation
- Discount Rate
- Economic Analysis
- Economic Life
- Equivalent uniform annual benefit (EUAB)
- Equivalent uniform annual cost (EUAC)
- Future Value
- Net present value
- Opportunity Costs
- Payback periods
- Present Value
- Rate of return
- Taxes
- Time value of money

Key Points for Review

❖ **Types of Costs**
   - Opportunity costs
   - Sunk costs
   - Book costs
   - Incremental costs

❖ **Changes in Costs**
   - Inflation

- ✓ Money supply
- ✓ Exchange rates
- ✓ Demand-pull inflation
- ✓ Cost-push inflation
- o Deflation
- o Escalation
- o Currency variation

❖ **Governmental Cost Impacts**
- o Government regulations
- o Taxes
  - ✓ Value added tax (VAT)
  - ✓ Effective tax rates
  - ✓ Marginal tax rates
  - ✓ Investment tax credits
- o Depletion
- o Depreciation methods
  - ✓ Straight-line method (SL)
  - ✓ Double-declining balance method (DDB)
  - ✓ Sum-of-years digits method (SOYD)
  - ✓ Modified accelerated cost recovery system (MACRS) – US only
  - ✓ Units of production (UOP)

❖ **Economic Analysis Techniques**
- o Time value of money
  - ✓ Net present value method
  - ✓ Capitalized cost method
  - ✓ Equivalent uniform annual cost or benefit method
  - ✓ Rate of return analysis
  - ✓ Benefit-cost ratio analysis method
  - ✓ Payback period method

Check on Learning

1. _____ represents the foregone benefit by choosing one alternative over another.

    A. Book costs
    B. Sunk costs
    C. Opportunity costs
    D. Incremental costs

2. A cost that represents funds already spent by virtue of past decisions is:

    A. Opportunity cost
    B. Sunk cost
    C. Book cost
    D. Inflation

3. Book costs represent the value of an item as reflected _____.

    A. In the firm's books
    B. On the cash flows
    C. In the economic analysis decisions
    D. In the incremental costs

4. The rise in the price level of a good or service or market basket of goods and/or services is called

    _____.

    A. Currency variation
    B. Deflation
    C. Escalation
    D. Inflation

5. _____ is a technique to accommodate price increases or decreases during the life of the contract.

    A. Taxes
    B. Escalation
    C. Investment tax credits
    D. Depreciation

6. ABC Construction Company owns a crane with an original cost of $500,000 and an estimated salvage value of $200,000. Its life is estimated to be 15 years. Using straight-line (SL) method, calculate the depreciation of this asset.

    A. $20,000
    B. $33,333
    C. $13,500
    D. $50,000

7. ABC Construction Company owns a small tractor with an original cost of $10,000 and an estimated salvage value of $2,000. Its life is estimated to be 5 years. Using double-declining balance (DDB), in what year will the small tractor be fully depreciated?

    A. 5
    B. 4
    C. 2
    D. 1

8. A cross-country highway is built for $200,000,000 and will have maintenance costs of $500,000 per year. At 10 percent interest, what is the capitalized cost of perpetual service?

    A. $550,000,000
    B. $205,000,000
    C. $220,000,000
    D. $500,000,000

9. Two new highway systems are being considered for construction. Project West has a NPV (net present value) of benefits $30,000,000 and NPV of costs is $20,000,000. Project Southwest has a NPV of benefits $55,000,000 and NPV of costs is $45,000,000.

    Using the benefit-cost ratio analysis method, which highway system should be built?

    A. Project West should be built
    B. Project Southwest should be built
    C. Both highway systems should be built at the same time
    D. Neither highway system should be considered at all

10. As a cost professional, you are requested to perform project screening in ten minutes. Which one of following projects is worthy of further review?

    A. Project A requires $50 million investment, resulting in $20 million in benefits
    B. Project B requires $30 million investment, resulting in $14 million in benefits
    C. Project C requires $40 million investment, resulting in $15 million in benefits
    D. Project D requires $20 million investment, resulting in $3 million in benefits

Solutions

1. C   Opportunity costs
         Refer to Chapter 7, "Opportunity Costs" topic

2. B   Sunk costs
         Refer to Chapter 7, "Sunk Costs" topic

3. A   In the firm's books
         Refer to Chapter 7, "Book Costs" topic

4. D   Inflation
         Refer to Chapter 7, "Inflation" topic

5. B   Escalation
         Refer to Chapter 7, "Escalation" topic

6. A

    D = depreciation charge
    C = asset original cost
    S = salvage value
    N = asset depreciable life (years)

    $D = (C - S) / N$
    $D = (500,000 - 200,000) / 15$
    $D = 300,000/15$
    $D = \$20,000$
         Refer to Chapter 7, "Straight-line Depreciation" topic

7. B

    D = depreciation charge
    C = asset original cost
    BV_r = book value of asset at end of rth year
    BV_0 = book value at beginning of year 1 = C
    N = asset depreciable life (years)
    $D = (2 / N) (BV_{r-1})$

Year	DDB	DDB Calculated $	Allowable Depreciation	Book Value at Year End
1	(2/5) (10,000)	4,000	4,000	6,000
2	(2/5) (6,000)	2,400	2,400	3,600
3	(2/5) (3,600)	1,440	1,440	2,160
4	(2/5) (2,160)	864	160*	2,000
5	(2/5) (2,000)	800	0	2,000
Total		**9,504**	**8,000**	**2,000**

Because the small tractor cannot be depreciated below its salvage value of $2,000, Year 4 will see a reduced allowable depreciation of the small tractor.

* Note: An asset cannot be depreciated below its salvage value. Thus the depreciation for year 4 is limited to only $160 to claim the maximum cumulative depreciation allowance of $8,000 ($10,000 - $2,000). Year 5 has no depreciation allowance.

Refer to Chapter 7, "Sum-of-years Digit Depreciation" topic

8.   B

Capitalized Cost= $200,000,000 + ($ 500,000 / 0.10)
= $200,000,000 + ($5,000,000)
= $205,000,000
Refer to Chapter 7, "Capitalized cost" topic

9.   A

Project West

B/C = $30,000,000 / $20,000,000
B/C = 1.5 B/C ratio

Project Southwest

B/C = $55,000,000 / $45,000,000
B/C = 1.22 B/C ratio

On the basis of the B/C analysis, both projects have B/C ratios greater than 1, and pass the initial screening test. The next step is performing incremental B/C ratio tests by evaluating the increased cost of Project Southwest against Project West.

Incremental B/C = ($55,000-$30,000) / ($45,000 - $20,000) = 1

The incremental B/C of 1 indicates a break even situation. In this situation, Project West is preferred because of the lower investment cost.

Refer to Chapter 7, "Benefit-cost Ratio Analysis Method" topic

10.   B

Based on the limited information and tight time constraint, using payback period method is the only viable economic analysis technique.

Project A Payback = B/C = $50 M/ $20M = 2.5 years
Project B Payback = B/C = $30 M/ $14M = 2.14 Years
Project A Payback = B/C = $40 M/ $15M = 2.67 Years
Project A Payback = B/C = $20 M/ $3M = 6.67 Years

Project B has the shortest payback period indicating fastest recovery of the capital investment.

Refer to Chapter 7, "Payback Period Method" topic

Chapter 8 – Activity-Based Cost Management

Gary Cokins

Introduction/Learning Objectives

The general ledger uses a chart of accounts, whereas Activity-Based Cost Management (ABC/M) uses a chart of activities. Expenses occur at the point of acquisition with third parties. This is when money (or obligation) exits the company. From the expenses, all costs calculated are representations of how those expenses flow through work activities and into outputs of the work. ABC/M ties each cost element to an activity and makes cost structure transparent. Low and non-value contributing activities can be reduced or eliminated to improve cost efficiency. The key learning objectives are:

- Understand why managers and employees are misled by arbitrary cost allocations with broad averages that violate the costing cause-and-effect principle.
- Understand how Activity-Based Cost Management (ABC/M) transforms spending expenses on resources (e.g., salaries) into calculated costs of processes, and their work activities that belong to them, and then into products, service-lines, channels and customers.
- Identify how cost drivers cause costs to occur.
- Understand how attributes are tags or scores that are attached to activities to suggest actions
- Understand how ABC/M is used in addition to strategic purposes, such as profit margin analysis, for cost management, productivity, and asset use.

Terms to Know

- Activity-based cost management (ABC/M)
- Chart of accounts
- Cost
- Cost re-assignment network
- Direct expenses
- Indirect expenses (also known as overhead or indirect costs)
- Overhead

Key Points for Review

- ❖ **Overhead Expenses are Displacing Direct Expenses**
  - ○ Standard costs
    - ✓ Service organizations measure this type of output related information
    - ✓ Problems are overhead is on top of cost components
    - ✓ Overhead is an indirect expense

- ❖ **Impact of diversity in products, service lines, channels and customers**
  - ○ Why indirect expenses (overhead) are displacing direct expenses?
    - ✓ Automation and technology replacing manual jobs
    - ✓ Greater variety of products and services, with more and different customers

- ✓ Introduction of greater variation and diversity creates complexity results that require more overhead
- ✓ The shift to overhead displacing direct labor reveals complexity. ABC/M points out where the complexity is and where it comes from

❖ **Activities are expressed with action verbs and trace expenses to outputs**

- o **Pitfalls of using traditional cost allocations of expenses**
  - ✓ Salary and fringe benefit make up sizeable portion of controllable expenses
  - ✓ These expenses are reported as lump-sum amounts without offering insight and content of employee work
  - ✓ Managers lack the tool to control and influence expenses

- o **Activity Based Cost Management (ABC/M)**
  - ✓ Translate the work activities into a general ledger of expenses
  - ✓ ABC/M is used for analysis
  - ✓ ABC/M is starting point for calculating costs for both processes and diverse outputs
  - ✓ ABC/M resolves deficiencies of traditional financial accounting
  - ✓ ABC/M is work-centric

- o **Expenses must be distinguished from costs**
  - ✓ All costs are calculated costs
  - ✓ Review assumptions that are involved in conversion and translation of expenses into costs
  - ✓ Expenses occur at point of acquisition with third parties, including employee wages
  - ✓ When money exits the company, the "value" does not change
  - ✓ From expenses, all costs calculated are representations of how these expenses flow through work activities

- o **Difference between ABC/M and the General Ledger and traditional cost allocations**
  - ✓ ABC/M describes activities using an action-verb-adjective-noun grammar convention, such as inspect defective products
  - ✓ ABC/M uses a chart of activities
  - ✓ ABC/M describes what it was spent for
  - ✓ ABC/M is work-centric
  - ✓ General Ledger uses a chart of accounts
  - ✓ Chart of Accounts is inaccurate for reporting business process
  - ✓ General Ledger is organized around separate departments or cost centers
  - ✓ General Ledger uses mapping to its hierarchical organization chart
  - ✓ General Ledger describes what was spent
  - ✓ General Ledger is transaction-centric

- o **Activity drivers trigger the workload**
  - ✓ Each activity reveals the content of work and gives insights to what drives cost fluctuation
  - ✓ All costs actually originate with customer or beneficiary of the work
  - ✓ ABC/M provides the additional information of analysis to the data
  - ✓ Cost assignment network enables ABC/M to calculate more accurate costs of work
  - ✓ Cost allocations are structured as a one source to many distributions or cost

- ❖ **ABC/M is a Cost Re-assignment Network**
  - o ABC/M assigns 100 percent of the costs into the final products, service lines, channels, customers, and business sustaining costs. The customers are the final cost objects; their existence ultimately creates the need for an expense and cost structure in the first place. Cost objects are the persons or things that benefit from incurring work activities.
    - ✓ Three modules connected by cost assignment paths
      - ▪ Resources: Capacity to perform work. Traced to work activities
      - ▪ Work activities: Where work is performed. Assigned to cost objects
      - ▪ Final cost objects: Broad variety of outputs and services where cost accumulated

- ❖ **Using the attributes of Activity Based Cost Management**
  - o Identify organization work activities
    - ✓ What can be eliminated
    - ✓ What is ineffectively accomplished
    - ✓ What is required to sustain the organization
    - ✓ What can be discretionary and potentially eliminated
    - ✓ Review and classify what would be a high-value-adding activity
    - ✓ Review and classify what would be a low-value-adding activity
    - ✓ Review level of importance as critical or postponable
    - ✓ Review level of performance as exceeds or below expectations

- ❖ **Local versus enterprise-wide ABC/M**
  - o Enterprise-wide application: for strategic purposes; focusing on where to look for problems and opportunities; calculating profit margin data at all levels
    - ✓ A large parent (enterprise) ABC/M model is subdivided into its component children (local or subsets of organization) ABC/M models
    - ✓ Local or subsets of organization application: for tactical purposes; focusing on process and productivity improvement
      - ▪ Unit of costs of output made visible into modeling
      - ▪ Activity analysis—judges work based on the need, efficiency, and value

- ❖ **If ABC/M is the answer, what is the question?**
  - o Lower margin for decision errors
  - o ABC/M reveals where to remove waste, low-value-adding costs, and unused capacity, as well as understanding what drives their costs
  - o Better understanding of cause and effect connections
  - o Knowing real costs for outputs, product costs, and the "cost-to-serve"
  - o Degree of alignment of cost structure with organization's mission and strategy

- ❖ **ABC/M in advanced, mature users**
  - o Integration of the ABC/M output data with their decision support systems
  - o Learning skills and rules for resizing, reshaping, re-leveling, and otherwise readjusting their ABC/M systems
  - o Collecting and automatically importing data into the ABC/M system
  - o Automatically exporting the calculated data out of their ABC/M system

Check on Learning

1. Why have the indirect expenses (i.e., overhead) of most organizations been displacing the direct expenses as a relative portion of its cost structure?

    A. Machinery and automation has replaced manual work
    B. Computers and information technology has replaced manual work
    C. The expansion in diverse product lines and types of sales and distribution channels has caused complexity requiring more indirect expenses to manage the complexity
    D. White collar salaries have been rising faster than wages of front-line workers

2. How are "expenses" defined differently from "costs?"

    A. Expenses pertain only to employee expense reports
    B. In contrast to capital investments, expenses are only for items consumed within a year after being purchased
    C. There is no difference and the two terms are synonymous
    D. Expenses are when cash is paid out by the organization and costs are the calculated usage of the expense spending

3. What is the primary determinant influencing the accuracy of costs?

    A. The detail level of the general ledger cost codes
    B. The structure of the cost assignment network
    C. The quality of employee time sheets
    D. Having more than one activity cost driver

4. What are the ultimate final cost objects of a cost measurement system?

    A. Product and service line costs
    B. Customer and business sustaining costs
    C. Employee paychecks and vendor invoices
    D. Customer costs

5. How is a "local" ABC/M system different from an "enterprise-wide" ABC/M system?

    A. Local ABC/M is restricted to measure only product profitability
    B. Enterprise-wide ABC/M is intended to distribute cost reports primarily to department and cost center employees
    C. The purpose of local ABC/M reporting is mainly to drive process improvement and productivity
    D. Local ABC/M primarily feeds the pricing and quotation system

6. All the following statements are correct except:

   A. Expenses and costs are the same depending on the perspective of contractors or owners
   B. In ABC/M system, all costs are calculated representations of how expenses flow through work activities and into outputs of work
   C. The general ledger uses a chart of accounts
   D. ABC/M uses a chart of activities

7. Cost assignment network includes the following three modules:

   A. Resources, schedule, and final cost objects
   B. Resources, work activities, and schedule
   C. Resources, work activities, and final cost objects
   D. Work activities, schedule and final cost objects

8. All the following are high-value-adding activities except:

   A. Those that are critical steps that cannot be eliminated in a business process
   B. Those that are performed to resolve or eliminate quality problems
   C. Those that are performed as a result of a request or expectation of a satisfied customer
   D. Those that are performed to monitor quality problems

9. In terms of applying ABC/M, which one is incorrect?

   A. Process and productivity improvements are expected for the enterprise
   B. Process and productivity improvements are expected at the local level
   C. Enterprise-wide ABC/M can calculate profit margin data at all levels
   D. Local ABC/M is for tactical purposes

10. ABC/M provides visibility to organizations to:

   A. Remove waste
   B. Remove low-value adding activities
   C. Seek a better way to manage unused capacity
   D. All of the above

Solutions

1.   C   The expansion in diverse product lines and types of sales and distribution channels has caused complexity requiring more indirect costs to manage the complexity
> Refer to Chapter 8, "Impact of Diversity in Products, Service Lines, Channels, and Customers" topic

2.   D   Expenses are when cash is paid out by the organization, and costs are the calculated usage of the expense spending
> Refer to Chapter 8, "Activities Are Expressed With Action Verbs and Trace Expenses to Outputs" topic

3.   B   The structure of the cost assignment network
> Refer to Chapter 8, "ABC/M is a Cost Re-Assignment Network" topic

4.   B   Customer and business sustaining cost
> Refer to Chapter 8, "Using the Attributes of Activity-Based Cost Management" topic

5.   C   The purpose of local ABC/M reporting is mainly to drive process improvement and productivity
> Refer to Chapter 8, "Local vs. Enterprise-Wide ABC/M" topic

6.   A   Expenses and costs are the same depending on the perspective of contractors or owners
> Refer to Chapter 8, "Activities Are Expressed With Action Verbs and Trace Expenses to Outputs" topic

7.   C   Resources; work activities and final cost objects
> Refer to Chapter 8, "ABC/M is a Cost Re-Assignment Network" topic

8.   D   Are performed to monitor quality problems
> Refer to Chapter 8, "Local vs. Enterprise-Wide ABC/M" topic

9.   A   Process and productivity improvements are expected for the enterprise
> Refer to Chapter 8, "Local vs. Enterprise-Wide ABC/M" topic

10.   D   ABC/M provides visibility to organization to remove waste, low-value-adding activities and manage unused capacity
> Refer to Chapter 8, "Local vs. Enterprise-Wide ABC/M" topic

SECTION 2 – COST

Chapter 9 – Cost Estimating

Larry R. Dysert, CCP CEP DRMP FAACE AACE Hon. Life

Introduction/Learning Objectives

Cost estimating is of integral importance to the quality of the cost and scheduling program on any project. The integrity of the cost estimate is of paramount importance to the success of a project and this is ensured by the use of the appropriate cost estimating methodology. The cost estimate becomes the basis for setting up the cost budget, resources and the ensuing progress and schedule monitoring processes during project execution. To achieve this, a cost estimating basis/framework is necessary. The key learning objectives are:

- Understand the classification of cost estimates.
- Understand some of the common methodologies used in preparing cost estimates.
- Relate estimate accuracy to the level of scope information and methodologies used in preparing cost estimates.
- Understand how to apply risk analysis to determine contingency in an estimate.
- Understand how to present and review estimates.
- Apply the knowledge gained to specific project estimating situations.

Terms to Know

- Allowances
- Basis of estimate
- Bill of materials
- Budget
- Bulk materials
- Cash flow
- Code of accounts
- Constructability
- Contingency
- Cost
- Cost category
- Cost, design
- Cost estimate
- Cost estimating
- Direct costs
- Direct field costs
- Direct labor
- Escalation
- Fabricated materials
- Indirect field costs
- Indirect labor

- Inside battery limits (ISBL)
- Manufacturing cost
- Outside battery limits (OSBL)
- Overhead
- Price
- Productivity
- Project
- Quantification
- Risk
- Risk management
- Scope
- Take-offs
- Work breakdown structure (WBS)

Key Points for Review

❖ **Estimate classifications**
  - Class 5 – Least detailed
  - Class 4
  - Class 3
  - Class 2
  - Class 1 – Most detailed

❖ **Estimate characteristics**
  - Degree of project definition
  - End usage of the estimate
  - Estimating methodology
  - Estimating accuracy
  - Effort required to produce the estimate

❖ **Estimating methodologies**
  - Conceptual estimating methodologies
    - ✓ End product units method
    - ✓ Physical dimensions method
    - ✓ Capacity factor method
    - ✓ Ratio or factor method
    - ✓ Parametric method

❖ **Deterministic (Detailed) estimating methodologies**
  - Prepare project estimate basis and schedule
  - Prepare Direct Field Cost (DFC) estimate
  - Prepare Indirect Field Cost (IFC) estimate
  - Prepare Home Office Cost (HOC) estimate
  - Prepare sales tax/duty estimates
  - Prepare escalation estimates
  - Prepare project fee estimate (for contractors)

- Prepare cost risk analysis/contingency determination
- Preview/validate estimate

❖ **Quantity take-offs**
- Quantifying the material and labor quantities associated with the project

❖ **Costing vs Pricing**
- Material costing/pricing
- Labor costing/pricing
    - ✓ Composite wage rate
    - ✓ Unit rate construction

❖ **Estimate allowances**
- Design allowance for engineered equipment
- Material take-off allowance
- Overbuy allowance
- Unrecoverable shipping damage allowance
- Allowance for undefined major items

❖ **Estimate accuracy**
- Estimate accuracy depends on the level of engineering complete

❖ **Contingency and risk analysis**
- Contingency is required because estimating is not an exact science
- Contingency exclusion
    - ✓ Significant changes in scope
    - ✓ Major unexpected work stoppages (strikes, etc.)
    - ✓ Disasters (hurricanes, tornadoes, etc.)
    - ✓ Excessive, unexpected inflation
    - ✓ Excessive, unexpected currency fluctuations

❖ **Structuring estimates**
- Material vs. Labor vs. Subcontracts
- Direct Costs vs. Indirect Costs vs. Home Office Costs
- Concrete vs. Structural Steel vs. Piping vs. Other Construction Disciplines

❖ **Estimate/schedule integration**
- Need close communication between estimator and schedule at appropriate high level WBS

❖ **Estimate reviews**
- Estimating team/Estimating department review
- Check the math

❖ **Basis of estimate**
- Design basis
- Planning basis
- Cost basis

- o Risk basis

❖ **Estimate validation**
- o Review estimate "metrics" report
- o Compare key benchmark ratios and factors versus historical values from similar projects

❖ **Presenting estimate**
- o Basis of Estimate (BOE)
- o Estimate Summaries
- o Estimate Detail
- o Estimate Benchmarking Report
- o Estimate Reconciliation Report
- o Estimate Backup

❖ **Estimating resources**
- o Engineering and design information
- o Conceptual estimating factors
- o Material cost and pricing information
- o Labor workhour charts and information
- o Labor productivity information
- o Labor wage rates, composite crew mixes, etc.
- o Other estimating factors and information

Check on Learning

1. An estimate prepared using cost/capacity factors would typically be classified as which type of estimate.

    A. Class 5 – Concept screen estimate
    B. Class 4 – Study estimate
    C. Class 3 – Budget estimate
    D. Class 2 – Control estimate

2. Assuming the cost for a 150 ton per day (TPD) waste-to-energy plant has been normalized for location and escalation. The adjusted cost for the 150 TPD plant is USD $80MM. For this type of project, the cost/capacity factor is taken as .65 based on historical cost relationships. What is the cost for a 90 TPD plant?

    A. USD $48.0MM
    B. USD $57.4MM
    C. USD $59.8MM
    D. USD $111.5MM

3. Which of the following is not true regarding a "detailed" estimate?

    A. Each component of the project scope definition is quantitatively surveyed and priced using the most realistic unit prices available
    B. It requires a substantial amount of time and money to prepare
    C. It uses a conceptual estimating methodology
    D. It is typically the most accurate of the various estimating methodologies

4. Which of the following is true regarding "allowances"?

    A. Allowances are never required in an estimate
    B. Allowances are most often used when preparing detailed or deterministic estimates
    C. Allowances are always calculated based as a percentage of some other detailed cost components of the estimate
    D. Allowances are the amounts added to an originally defined point estimate to achieve a given probability of not overrunning the estimate

5. What is the primary goal of an estimate review?

    A. To predict the probable cost of a project
    B. To verify the estimating software used in preparing the estimate
    C. To ensure that the actual costs will not overrun the estimate
    D. To determine that a high quality and sufficiently accurate estimate has been prepared

6. Which of the following is the primary characteristic that determines the class of estimate being prepared?

A. The end usage of the estimate
B. The degree of project definition
C. The effort required to prepare the estimate
D. The estimating methodology

7. Estimating the cost of construction of a proposed hotel based on the average cost per hotel room of a recently completed hotel involves which estimating methodology?

   A. Capacity-factor method
   B. Physical-dimensions method
   C. End-product units method
   D. Parametric method

8. The basic steps of preparing a cost estimate include all of the following except?

   A. Understanding the scope of the activity to quantify the resources required
   B. Evaluating project alternatives
   C. Applying costs to the resources
   D. Applying pricing adjustments

9. Estimate accuracy tends to improves as?

   A. The amount of contingency included in the estimate increases
   B. The amount of contingency included in the estimate decreases
   C. The level of detail in the estimate increases
   D. The level of project definition used to prepare the estimate improves

10. Which of the following is a key element of estimate-schedule integration?

    A. Schedule impacts may directly affect labor productivity adjustments in the estimate, as well as labor and material pricing
    B. There should be a one-to-one relationship between estimate cost items and schedule activities
    C. Changes in the project schedule only affect the amount of escalation to be included in the estimate
    D. The estimate is usually not prepared in correlation with a specific schedule

Solutions

1.   A   Class 5—Concept screening estimate
                  Refer to Chapter 9, "Estimate Classifications" topic & Figure 9.2

2.   B   USD \$80MM X $(90/150)^{.65}$ = USD\$57.4MM
                  Refer to Chapter 9, "Capacity Factor Method" topic

3.   C   Uses a conceptual estimating methodology
                  Refer to Chapter 9, "Estimate Classifications" topic & Figure 9.2

4.   B   Allowances are most often used when preparing detailed or deterministic estimates
                  Refer to Chapter 9, "Estimate Allowances" topic

5.   D   To determine that a high quality and sufficiently accurate estimate has been prepared
                  Refer to Chapter 9, "Estimate Review" topic

6.   B   The degree of project definition
                  Refer to Chapter 9, "Estimate Classifications" topic

7.   C   End-product units method
                  Refer to Chapter 9, "End Product Units Method" topic

8.   B   Evaluate project alternatives
                  Refer to Chapter 9, "Introduction" topic

9.   D   The level of project definition used to prepare the estimate improves
                  Refer to Chapter 9, "Estimate Classifications" topic

10.   A   Schedule impacts may directly affect labor productivity adjustments in the estimate as well as labor and material pricing
                  Refer to Chapter 9, "Estimate/Cost/Schedule Integration" topic

Chapter 10 – Process Product Manufacturing

Kenneth K. Humphreys, PE CCP FAACE

Introduction/Learning Objectives

All operating and manufacturing costs must be considered to determine the profitability of a process in the manufacturing environment. These costs are treated differently for purposes of calculating taxes and profitability. The key learning objectives are:

- Understand how to determine the operating and manufacturing costs of a continuous process on a conceptual basis.
- Distinguish between direct and indirect costs in manufacturing as compared to construction.
- Relate operating costs at full production to reduced costs at less than full plant capacity.
- Understand depreciation rules and their relationship to operating and manufacturing costs.

Terms to Know

- Direct Costs
- Distribution Costs
- Fixed Costs
- General and Administrative (G & A) Expenses
- Indirect Costs
- Semi-variable Costs

Key Points for Review

- ❖ **Prerequisite of Preparing Operating or Manufacturing Cost Estimate**
  - o Process flow sheets with information such as quantity, composition, temperature, pressure, etc.
  - o Estimating form serving as a check list
  - o Obtaining company internal data for similar process
  - o External published data sources but use this data with caution

- ❖ **Variable Costs**
  - o Raw materials
  - o Utilities
  - o Royalties (if applicable)
  - o Packaging (if applicable)
  - o Marketing
  - o Catalysts and chemicals

- ❖ **Semi-variable Costs**
  - o Direct labor
  - o Supervision
  - o General expenses

- Plant overhead

❖ **Fixed Costs**
- Royalties (if applicable)
- Plant and equipment
- Depreciation
- Property taxes
- Insurance

❖ **Four Ways to Handle Royalties**
- Capitalized cost if it is paid in a lump sum
- Fixed cost if it is paid in equal annual increments
- Variable cost if a fee is paid based on per unit of production
- Semi-variable cost if it is paid in a sliding scale (based on per unit of production but decreases as production increases (or hits a target quantity))

❖ **Understand How to Calculate:**
- Minimum return point
- Breakeven point
- Shutdown point

❖ **Raw Material Costs**
- External raw material costs
- Internal raw material costs transferred at market value or company book value

❖ **By-product Credits and Debits**
- Estimate salable by-product credit from the anticipated selling prices less costs of processing, packaging, selling and transporting to market
- By-product debits include all costs to remove, eliminate, or reduce wastes and pollutants

❖ **Utility Costs (Total Consumption and Demand)**
- Electricity
- Natural gas
- Water
- Fuel
- Equipment losses
- Mobile equipment fuels and lubricants

❖ **Labor Costs**
- Straight time
- Overtime premium and holiday premiums (if required by production demands)
- Supervision
- Overhead

❖ **Maintenance Costs (Part of Semi-variable Costs)**
- Direct maintenance labor
- Direct maintenance supervision

- o Maintenance materials
- o Contract maintenance

❖ **Operating Supplies and Overhead Costs**
- o Operating supplies include lubricant oil, wiping cloths, blades, cutting edges, etc.
- o Overhead (burden) costs are associated with payroll or general and administrative expenses
- o Expenses of testing and research laboratories

❖ **General Work Expense (Factory Overhead)**
- o Indirect cost of operating a plant or factory and is dependent on both investment and labor
- o Excluding general expense (i.e., marketing or sales cost) and administrative cost

❖ **Depreciation (Treated as Fixed, Indirect Cost)**
- o Straight-line method
- o Double-declining balance method
- o Accelerated cost recovery system (ACRS) (for US installations only)
- o Modified accelerated cost recovery system (MACRS) (for US installations only)

❖ **Distribution Costs**
- o Cost of containers
- o Transportation costs
- o Applicable labor and overhead for packaging and shipping
- o May include shipment-insurance costs

Check on Learning

1. The preferred basis to estimate operating cost is:

    A. Daily basis
    B. Unit-of-production basis
    C. Annual basis
    D. Hourly

2. Annual basis for operating cost estimates is preferred because _____.

    A. It is directly usable in profitability analysis
    B. It "damps out" season variations
    C. It is readily convertible to the other bases, daily cost and unit-of-production
    D. All of the above

3. Which of the costs listed below would be considered as semi-variable costs?

    A. Property taxes
    B. Raw materials
    C. Direct labor
    D. Royalties

4. Which of the costs listed below would be considered as fixed costs?

    A. Depreciation
    B. Utilities
    C. Plant overhead
    D. Marketing

5. At which point will income exactly equal total operating cost?

    A. Shutdown point
    B. Minimum-production rate
    C. Break-even point
    D. Full-production point

6. In a manufacturing operation, at 100 percent of capacity, annual costs are as follows:

    Fixed expenses $5,203,440
    Variable expenses $7,091,040
    Semi-variable expenses $6,217,750
    Sales $26,385,480

    Given that semi-variable expenses at zero production equal 30% of such expenses at 100% of capacity, the respective shutdown and break-even points would be:

A. 47.3% shutdown point and 12.5% break-even point
B. 12.5% shutdown point and 47.3% break-even point
C. 12.5% shutdown point and 36.6% break-even point
D. Cannot be determined from the given information

7. A pharmaceutical company plans to install USD$66,000,000 worth of new equipment this year. The equipment is estimated to have a salvage value of USD$5,500,000 at the end of its 10-year useful life. What is the IRS-approved depreciation allowance for Year 5 (based on U.S. Tax Law)?

   A. $16,163,400
   B. $11,543,400
   C. $8,243,400
   D. $5,893,800

8. A process plant is considering purchasing an additional heat exchanger to lower the feedstock temperature in a process. The heat exchanger and related work will cost $100,000 with a salvage value of $10,000 and the end of its 8-year useful life. With straight-line depreciation, what is the book value of this heat exchanger at the end of Year 3?

   A. $37,500
   B. $33,750
   C. $66,250
   D. $62,500

9. A new type of process control system has a first cost of $250,000 and an estimated salvage value of $50,000 at the end of its economic life of 5 years. Assume that for accounting purposes, rather than tax purposes, that the process plant utilizes sum-of-the-year's digits method for depreciation calculations. What is the depreciation in Year 3?

   A. $48,000
   B. $60,000
   C. $50,000
   D. $40,000

10. Which of the following is a non-cash outlay associated with a process manufacturing project?

   A. Interest expenses
   B. Corporate federal income taxes
   C. Operating expenses such as labor and material
   D. Depreciation expenses

11. An overhead cost:

   A. Is in direct proportion to the labor intensity involved in the product
   B. Is a non-controllable cost
   C. Is a required cost; but it cannot be traced directly to a product or product item
   D. Depreciation expenses

12. Process Unit X costs USD$10,000 more than Unit Y. However, in use, Process Unit X averages 0.08 hours of maintenance labor per day versus Unit Y with an average of 0.14 hours of maintenance labor per day. Both Process Units X and Y have a 15-year useful life. Unit Y has a salvage value that is $2,000 less than that of Unit X. Maintenance costs per hour are $85.00 which is fully burdened including consumables and related tool costs, etc. It is anticipated that both Unit X and Unit Y will be utilized intermittently throughout the year. Given that all other factors (safety, quality, thru-put, etc.) are equal, beyond how many days of use is Unit X preferred over Unit Y?

    A. 45
    B. 56
    C. 105
    D. 131

Solutions:

1. C Annual basis
    Refer to Chapter 10, "Types of Operating Cost Estimates and Estimating Forms" topic

2. D All of the above
    Refer to Chapter 10, "Types of Operating Cost Estimates and Estimating Forms" topic

3. C Direct labor
    Refer to Chapter 10, "Cost of Operations at Less Than Full Capacity" topic

4. A Depreciation
    Refer to Chapter 10, "Cost of Operations at Less Than Full Capacity" topic

5. C Break-even point
    Refer to Chapter 10, "Fig 10.2"

6. B 12.5% shutdown point and 47.3% break-even point

    (All dollar values are $USD)

    $$\text{Shutdown point} = \frac{nR}{S-V-(1-n)\,R}$$

    $$\frac{0.30 \times \$6,217,750}{\$26,385,480 - \$7,091,040 - (1-0.30) \times \$6,217,750}$$

    $$\frac{\$1,865,325}{\$19,294,440 - (0.70) \times \$6,217,750}$$

    $$\frac{\$1,865,325}{\$19,294,440 - \$4,352,425}$$

    $$\frac{\$1,865,325}{\$14,942,015} = 0.1248 \text{ or } \textbf{12.5\% of capacity}$$

    $$\text{Breakeven point} = \frac{(F+nR)}{S-V-(1-n)\,R}$$

    $$\frac{\$5,203,440 + (0.30 \times \$6,217,750)}{\$26,385,480 - \$7,091,040 - (1-0.30) \times \$6,217,750}$$

    $$\frac{\$5,203,440 + \$1,865,325}{\$19,294,440 - (0.70) \times \$6,217,750}$$

$$\frac{\$7,068,765}{\$19,294,440 - \$4,352,425}$$

$\frac{\$7,068,765}{\$14,942,015} = 0.473$ or **47.3% of capacity**

        Refer to Chapter 10, "Fig 10.2; equations 10.1 & 10.2"

7.   D $5,893,800

First choose the MACRS (Modified Accelerated Cost Recovery System) to calculate the depreciation (1986 US Tax Reform Act).

MACRS and ACRS (Accelerated Cost Recovery System) do not consider salvage value. Use Table 10.5 MACRS deduction rates from S&K 6. Choose the "7-Year Column" because it is 10 years or more, but less than 16 years.

Year 1	0.1429 % X $66,000,000 = $9,431,400
Year 2	0.2449 % X $66,000,000 = $16,163,400
Year 3	0.1749 % X $66,000,000 = $11,543,400
Year 4	0.1249 % X $66,000,000 = $8,243,400
Year 5	0.0893 % X $66,000,000 = $5,893,800

        Refer to Chapter 10, "Modified Accelerated Cost Recovery System" topic

8.   C $66,250

$100,000 cost - $10,000 salvage value = $90,000 depreciable amount
$90,000/8-Year Life = $11,250 depreciation allowance per year
At end of Year 3, three years of depreciation has been taken (3 x $11,250 = $33,750)
$100,000 - $33,750 = $66,250

        Refer to Chapter 10, "Depreciation" topic & Equation 10.6

9.   D $40,000

Sum-of-the-year's digits (SOYD) = $(n/2)(n + 1) = (5/2)(5 + 1) = 15$
Year 3 SOYD depreciation = $(3/15)(\$250,000 - \$50,000) = \$40,000$

        Refer to Chapter 10, "Depreciation" & Equation 10.8

10.   D   Depreciation expenses

Depreciation expenses are non-cash costs that result from investments in such capital goods as plant and equipment. Governments, in most countries around the world, in order to encourage such investments, allow firms to write off the investment on a yearly basis as an offset to their income taxes. Therefore no money actually changes hands since this is a "book" cost.

        Refer to Chapter 10, "Depreciation" topic

11.   C   Is a required cost but cannot be traced directly to a product or product item

If a cost could be directly traced to a product then it should be included in that cost category but typically when there are issues of traceability, the cost is then categorized in the overhead area.

        Refer to Chapter 10, "Operating supplies and overhead costs" topic

12.　　C　　105 days

$-\$10,000 + \$2,000 + (0.14 - 0.08)(\$85.00)(15)(X) = 0$

$-\$8,000 + (76.5)(X) = 0$

$X = \$8,000 / 76.5$

$X = 105$ days

Refer to Chapter 10, "Cost of operations at less than full capacity" topic

Chapter 11 – Discrete Part Manufacturing

Dr. Robert C. Creese, PE CCP

Introduction/Learning Objectives

Various manufacturing philosophies are used in discrete manufacturing, or the production of separate and individual pieces that are produced in small amounts. The key learning objectives are:

- Understand the fundamentals of basic operations in discrete part manufacturing.
- Comprehend the discrete part manufacturing philosophies.
- Identify the basic cost terms and relationships in discrete manufacturing.
- Understand cost-estimating-item components in discrete manufacturing.
- Recognize differences between time-based and quantity-based approaches to break-even analysis.
- Identify the four break-even points in discrete part manufacturing.
- Calculate the four break-even points in discrete part manufacturing.

Terms to Know

- Administrative Expense
- Contingency
- Cost
- Cost Estimating
- Costing (Cost Accounting)
- Direct Burden Expenses
- Direct Costs
- Direct Engineering Costs
- Direct Labor Costs
- Direct Material Costs
- Factory Expenses
- Indirect Burden Expenses
- Indirect Costs
- Indirect Engineering Costs
- Indirect Labor Costs
- Indirect Material Costs
- Marketing, Selling And Distribution Expenses
- Mark-Up Rate (Profit)
    - Gross Profit
    - Operating Profit
    - Net Profit
- Production Cost

Key Points for Review

❖ **Discrete-part manufacturing philosophies**
  ○ Computer-aided process planning
  ○ Concurrent engineering
  ○ Group technology
  ○ Just-In-Time
  ○ Lean manufacturing
  ○ Materials requirements planning
  ○ Supply chain management
  ○ Total quality management
  ○ Total cost management

❖ **Basic cost relationships**
  ○ Prime cost
  ○ Manufacturing cost
  ○ Production cost
  ○ Total cost
  ○ Selling price

❖ **Cost estimating guide form**

❖ **Break-even analysis**
  ○ Cost basis
    ✓ Time-based
    ✓ Quantity-based
  ○ Break-even points
    ✓ Shutdown point
    ✓ Cost point
    ✓ Required return point
    ✓ Required return after taxes point

Check on Learning

1. The manufacturing philosophy to shorten lead times, reduce costs, and reduce waste is known as:

    A. Supply-chain management
    B. Material-requirements planning (MRP)
    C. Group technology
    D. Lean manufacturing

2. The manufacturing philosophy that identifies and exploits the underlying sameness of component parts and manufacturing processes is known as:

    A. Supply-chain management
    B. Material-requirements planning (MRP)
    C. Group technology
    D. Lean manufacturing

3. The mark-up rate for a product is 20 percent, and the total costs are $100,000. What should the selling price be?

    A. $100,000
    B. $120,000
    C. $125,000
    D. $400,000

4. The data for the following product was obtained for an order of 30,000 parts:

Direct Material Costs	$50,000
Factory Expenses	$5,000
Direct Labor Costs	$40,000
Administrative Expenses	$15,000
Selling and Distribution Expenses	$24,000
Contingency Costs	$10,000
Mark-up Rate	10 percent
Units Produced	30,000

    4a. What is the prime cost?

    A. $55,000
    B. $90,000
    C. $110,000
    D. $120,000

    4b. What is the manufacturing cost?

    A. $90,000
    B. $95,000

C. $105,000
D. $110,000

4c. What is the total cost?

A. $110,000
B. $144,000
C. $160,000
D. $190,000

5. Quantity based break-even:

Item	$/unit	$	Decimal
Sales Revenue	10		
Manufacturing Costs			
Material	3		
Labor	1		
Indirect	2	600	
Overhead		1,400	
Required Return		800	
Tax Rate (20%)			0.20

5a. What is the shutdown point in units of production?

A. 100
B. 150
C. 500
D. 700

5b. What is the cost point in units of production?

A. 150
B. 500
C. 700
D. 750

5c. What is the required return point in units of production?

A. 150
B. 500
C. 700
D. 750

5d. What is the required return after taxes point in units of production?

    A. 500
    B. 700
    C. 750
    D. 800

6. Time based break-even analysis:

Item	$/hr	$	Decimal
Sales Revenue		40,000	
Manufacturing Costs			
Material		15,000	
Labor	10		
Indirect		5,000	
Overhead	10		
Required Return	12		
Tax Rate (40%)			0.40

6a. What is the shutdown point in hours?

    A. 2,500
    B. 2,000
    C. 1,250
    D. 1,000

6b. What is the cost point in hours?

    A. 2,000
    B. 1,250
    C. 1,000
    D. 625

6c. What is the required return point in hours?

    A. 2,000
    B. 1,250
    C. 1,000
    D. 625

6d. What is the required return-after-taxes point in hours?

    A. 2,000
    B. 1,250
    C. 625
    D. 500

7. The manufacturing philosophy which requires that the supplies (raw materials) are delivered when required and inventory costs are theoretically driven to zero, as there is no inventory, is best known as:

   A. Concurrent inventory
   B. Just-in-Time
   C. Material-requirements planning
   D. Computer-aided manufacturing

8. All expenditures, other than direct labor, direct material, and direct engineering that can be directly allocated and charged to the product are known as _____. This can include tooling such as jigs and fixtures, patterns, etc., that can be charged to the specific product.

   A. Direct burden expense
   B. Overhead expense
   C. Plant and equipment expense
   D. Overhead engineering expense

9. In the "Ladder of Costs" for discrete part manufacturing, selling and distribution expenses would be added onto what component to yield total cost?

   A. Production cost
   B. Manufacturing cost
   C. Factory cost
   D. Prime cost

10. Earnings of income after all the expenses (selling, administrative, depreciation) have been deducted is known as:

   A. Operating profit
   B. Gross profit
   C. Net profit
   D. After-tax profit

Solutions

1. D Lean Manufacturing—Lean manufacturing is a manufacturing philosophy to shorten lead times, reduce costs and reduce waste. This philosophy is implemented by reducing waste through scrap reduction, improving yields and developing new products from waste stream materials, improving employee performance, skills, and satisfaction via training, recognition, and employee involvement and empowerment, and investing capital to improve processes, process rates, and capabilities. Lean manufacturing is not "mean" manufacturing and it is not a short term process, but is a continuous improvement process.
    Refer to Chapter 11, "Discrete part manufacturing philosophies" topic

2. C Group Technology—Group technology is a manufacturing philosophy that identifies and exploits the underlying sameness of component parts and manufacturing process. There are two primary approaches which are: classifying parts into families that have similar design features and classifying parts into families which have similar processing operations. This permits the standardization of parts in the design process and in the second case, production of parts as families by permitting cell formation and reducing the set-up times via fewer set-up changes.
    Refer to Chapter 11, "Discrete part manufacturing philosophies" topic

3. C Mark-up = $100,000 x (20%/ (100 − 20%)) = $25,000
    Selling price = total costs + mark-up
    Selling price = $100,000 + $25,000 = $125,000
    Refer to Chapter 11, Equations 11. 5, 11.6, and 11.7

4a. B Prime Cost = direct material cost + direct labor cost + direct engineering cost + direct expenses
    Prime Cost = $50,000 + $40,000 + $0 + $0
    Prime Cost = $90,000
    Refer to Chapter 11, Equation 11.1

4b. C Manufacturing cost = prime cost + factory expense + contingency costs*
    Manufacturing cost = $90,000 + $5,000 + $10,000
    Manufacturing cost = $105,000
    Refer to Chapter 11, Equation 11.2

    * **Note**: contingency costs would be part of the manufacturing costs as they would be part of the prime cost or factory expense in most instances, but since these were listed separately they would be added to the prime cost. They are typically from design changes.

4c. B Total Cost = production cost + marketing, selling, and distribution expenses or
    Total Cost = manufacturing cost + administrative expenses + marketing, selling and distribution expenses

Total Cost = $105,000 + $15,000 + $24,000
Total Cost = $144,000
                Refer to Chapter 11, Equation 11.4

5a.   B   Shutdown Point
            Revenue = Production costs
            10 x = 3x + 1x + 2x + 600
            10 x = 6x + 600
            x = 150
                    Refer to Chapter 11, "Production quantity based calculations" topic

5b.   B   Cost Point
            Revenue = Production costs + marketing, selling, and distribution expenses=Total costs
            10x = 6x + 600 + 1,400 = 6x + 2,000
            4x = 2,000
            x = 500
                    Refer to Chapter 11, "Production quantity based calculations" topic

5c.   C   Required Return Point
            Revenue = Total Costs + Required Return
            10x = 6x + 2,000 + 800
            4x = 2,800
            X = 700
                    Refer to Chapter 11, "Production quantity based calculations" topic

5d.   C   Required Return-after-Taxes
            Revenue = Total Costs + Required Return + Taxes on Required Return
            10x = 6x + 2,000 + 800 + 800 x tax rate/(1.0 − tax rate)
            10x = 6x + 2,000 + 800[(1.0 − tax rate + tax rate)/(1.0 − tax rate)]
            10x = 6x + 2,000 + 800/(1.0 − tax rate) **
            10x = 6x + 2,000 + 800/(1.0 − 0.2) = 6x + 2,000 + 1,000
            10x = 6x + 3,000
            4x = 3,000
            x = 750

            **Note: Need 1000 return-before-taxes at 20% to get 800 return-after-taxes.
                    Refer to Chapter 11, "Production quantity based calculations" topic

6a.   B   Shutdown Point
            Revenue = Production Costs
            $ 40,000 = $15,000 + 10y + $5,000
            $ 40,000 = $20,000 + 10y
            10y = $20,000
            y = 2,000 hours
                    Refer to Chapter 11, "Time based calculations" topic

6b.   C   Cost Point
Revenue = Production Costs + marketing, selling, and distribution expenses = Total Costs
$40,000 = $20,000 + 10y + 10y = $20,000 + 20y
20y = $20,000
y = 1,000 hours
    Refer to Chapter 11, "Time based calculations" topic

6c.   D   Required Return Point
Revenue = Total Costs + Required Return
$40,000 = $20,000 + 20y + 12y
32y = $20,000
y = 625 hours
    Refer to Chapter 11, "Time based calculations" topic

6d.   D   Required Return Point after Taxes
Revenue = Total Costs + Required Return + Taxes for Required Return
$40,000 = $20,000 + 20y + 12y + 12y x tax rate / (1 − tax rate)
$40,000 = $20,000 + 20y + 12y /(1-tax rate) = $20,000 + 20y + 12y/(1 − 0.4)
$40,000 = $20,000 + 20y + 12y/(0.6) = $20,000 + 20 y + 20 y = $20,000 + 40 y
40y = $20,000
y = 500 hours
    Refer to Chapter 11, "Time based calculations" topic

7.   B   Just-In-Time
    Refer to Chapter 11, "Breakeven point discussion" topic

8.   A   Direct burden expense
    Refer to Chapter 11, "Direct Costs" topic

9.   A   Production cost
    Refer to Chapter 11, "Basic cost relationship" topic & Figure 11.2

10.   A   Operating profit
    Refer to Chapter 11, "Mark-up rate" topic

SECTION 3 – PLANNING AND SCHEDULING

Chapter 12 – Project Planning

James A Bent, CCP
Jennifer Bates, CCP FAACE AACE Hon. Life
Pete Griesmyer, FAACE

Introduction/Learning Objectives

It is important to understand the significance of effective project planning as well as develop the ability and tool set to establish a project plan that includes the following:

- Work breakdown Structure (WBS) and required levels of schedule detail
- Known key/critical restraints and interfaces
- Key elements of project and construction preplanning include:
    1. Summarizing goals
    2. Time planning
    3. Cost planning
    4. Resource planning
    5. Quality planning
    6. Planning for change
- Constructability studies

The key learning objectives are:

- Understand the role of the project manager and the project planner in project planning.
- Understand planning strategies.
- Understand the importance of planning.
- Understand planning deliverables.

Terms to Know

- Baseline
- Budgeting
- Constraint
- Constructability
- Contingency
- CPM – Critical Path Method
- Critical path
- Planning
- Risk management
- Scheduling
- Scope
- Work breakdown structure (WBS)
- Work packages

Key Points for Review

- ❖ **Develop/establish a planning culture**
  - ○ Prepare clear scope definition
  - ○ Team effort
  - ○ Resultant plan is well documented
  - ○ Plan a baseline for control
  - ○ Post-completion review

- ❖ **Importance of Planning**
  - ○ Maximize the opportunity
    - ✓ Use best information available
    - ✓ Activities are monitored and controlled against a referenced baseline
  - ○ Increase the knowledge base for the next opportunity
    - ✓ Maintain records for feedback to increase knowledge base for next planning action
    - ✓ Learning curve in action
    - ✓ Future planning much easier
    - ✓ Avoid "reinventing the wheel"
    - ✓ Avoid wasting time and money

- ❖ **Planning Process Steps**
  - ○ Setting objectives
  - ○ Gathering information
  - ○ Determining feasible alternative plans
  - ○ Choosing the best alternative
  - ○ Communicating the plan
  - ○ Implementing the plan
  - ○ Adjusting the plan to meet new conditions as they arise
  - ○ Reviewing the effectiveness of the plan against attainment of objectives

- ❖ **Planning Tools Available**
  - ○ Commercial handbooks and software programs
  - ○ Standard company policies and procedures
  - ○ Model plans adopted for current use
  - ○ Checklist to avoid overlooking key items
  - ○ Code of accounts

- ❖ **Major Elements of Planning**

- ❖ **Project objectives are prioritized, documented and communicated**
  - ○ Establishes a process of clear priorities that allows multiple groups to work in harmony
  - ○ Establish the idea of working together, project commitment, cost consciousness and personnel satisfaction as deliverables
  - ○ Execution plan is formal and written
  - ○ Effective team building has been established

- ❖ **Scope definition control**
  - ○ Establish project discipline and design control to prevent or identify scope changes
    - ✓ Project Information systems
  - ○ Establish effective interface with stakeholders, operations and maintenance for scope approval
  - ○ Scope is well defined before start of detailed engineering
  - ○ Decisions on scope are made in a timely manner
  - ○ Establishment of cost and schedule baselines: work breakdown structure, logic diagrams, risk analysis, estimating
  - ○ Change control process is identified and implemented

- ❖ **Constructability planning**
  - ○ An evaluation of the physical sequence of construction work to produce the lowest cost
  - ○ It is an integral part of project execution
  - ○ Front end planning incorporates construction input
  - ○ "Construction driven" scheduling as key to CPM program

- ❖ **Summarize goals and the scope of work**
  - ○ Clearly understood and agreed upon
  - ○ Segment into manageable parts using a WBS
  - ○ Plan each part in detail
  - ○ Combine parts
  - ○ Test total against goals

- ❖ **Time Planning**
  - ○ Accomplish goals in established time period
  - ○ Divide total effort into component parts
  - ○ Array in order of accomplishment
  - ○ Assign durations
  - ○ Determine total time requirement

- ❖ **Cost Planning**
  - ○ Divide into component parts
  - ○ Time phase according to schedule
  - ○ Sum to total budget

- ❖ **Resource Planning**
  - ○ Personnel
  - ○ Support equipment and tools
  - ○ Permanent materials
  - ○ Installed equipment
  - ○ Expendable supplies

- ❖ **Quality Planning**

- ❖ **Post Completion Review**

❖ **Planning for Change**
- o Contingency planning
- o Alternate plans
- o Cost and schedule contingency

Check on Learning

1. Planning can be defined as:

    A. Influencing the future by making decisions based on missions, needs, and objectives
    B. The process of stating goals and determining the most effective way of reaching them
    C. Future-oriented decision process defining the actions and activities, the time and cost targets, and the performance milestones that will result in successfully achieving objectives
    D. All of the above

2. Establishing a planning culture...

    A. Minimizes the importance of management buy-in and support for the planning process
    B. Requires commitment by top management, continues with communication of that commitment to mid-level managers, and becomes rooted when every employee relates unequivocally with the company's goals
    C. Ensures that each organization has the authority to act independently of established policies when developing plans
    D. Is not beneficial to the goals of the company and the cost of establishing this culture should be avoided

3. Which of the following materials is NOT a key doctrine this review chapter is based upon?

    A. TCM Framework, 2nd Edition
    B. Visual TCM rollout
    C. Skills and Knowledge of Cost Engineering, 6th Edition, Chapter 12, Project Planning
    D. AACE International Recommended Practice 39R-06

4. Which of the following is NOT considered to be a non-schedule planning methodology?

    A. Sequencing and phasing
    B. Emergency reaction plans
    C. Heavy lift plans
    D. Site access plans

5. The major elements of planning are:

    A. Scope of work, time, cost, resource, quality, post completion review and change
    B. Scope of work, scheduling, cost, resource, quality and change
    C. Time, cost, resource, quality and change
    D. Scope of work, time, cost, resource, contingency and change

6. The baseline plan is the _____ output of the _____ planning process for a project.

    A. Initial, final
    B. Primary, initial
    C. Final, initial
    D. Logical, tertiary

7. When should schedule risk be evaluated in the planning process?

    A. Continually throughout the lifecycle of the project
    B. Before the project plan is finalized
    C. Once the entire scope of work has been incorporated
    D. All of the above

8. Which one of the following is NOT considered a major category when developing a project execution plan?

    A. The scope of the work to be completed
    B. The team communications plan
    C. How the work will be executed
    D. When the work will be carried out

9. Who is directly responsible for creating an environment that will enable project control to be properly exercised?

    A. The project stakeholder(s)
    B. The Project Controls Manager
    C. The Project Manager
    D. The Executive Director

10. The "path of construction" analysis is an evaluation of the physical sequence of construction to produce the lowest cost. Which of the following is NOT a major factor involved in this evaluation?

    A. Physical conditions of the construction site
    B. Weather conditions at the site during the construction period
    C. Key constraints such as material delivery dates, plant operations shut downs, or resource crew sizes
    D. Construction waste disposal logistics

Solutions

1.   D   All of the above
   > Refer to Chapter 12, "Introduction" topic

2.   B   Requires commitment by top management, continues with communication of that commitment to mid-level managers, and becomes rooted when every employee relates unequivocally with the company's goals
   > Refer to Chapter 12, "Establishing a planning culture" topic

3.   B   Visual TCM rollout
   > Refer to Chapter 12, "Introduction" topic

4.   A   Sequencing and phasing
   > Refer to Chapter 12, "Non-Schedule Planning Methodologies" topic

5.   A   Scope of work, time, cost, resource, quality, post completion review and change
   > Refer to Chapter 12, "Planning tools" topic

6.   C   Final, initial
   > Refer to Chapter 12, "Baseline Plan" topic

7.   D   All of the above
   > Refer to Chapter 12, "Risk Management Planning" topic

8.   B   The team communications plan
   > Refer to Chapter 12, "Execution Plan/Formal Written Program" topic

9.   C   The Project Manager
   > Refer to Chapter 12, "A Team and Cost Culture is Developed on the Project" topic

10.   D   Construction waste disposal logistics
    > Refer to Chapter 12, "Constructability planning" topic

Chapter 13 – Scheduling

Anthony J. Werderitsch, PE CCP CFCC FAACE AACE Hon. Life

Introduction/Learning Objectives

This chapter provides a basic understanding of scheduling for seasoned, as well as, new project staff and allows one to understand the process of schedule model development, monitoring, progress updating, and forecasting to communicate to all project team members. The key learning objectives are:

- Identify scheduling terms.
- Understand scheduling methods and techniques including each one's benefits and risks.
- Understand the most commonly used method and technique that will meet your project objectives.
- Understand Work Breakdown Structures (WBS) and the dependencies between work tasks to enhance team efficiencies.
- Apply overlapping schedule techniques and calculations that reflect real world management applications.
- Understand how to manage changes to the schedule.

Terms to Know

- Activity
- Arrow Diagramming Method (ADM)
- Bar Chart/Gantt Chart
- Calendars
- Constraints
- Early and Late dates (ES, EF, LS, and LF)
- Float
- Forward pass and backward pass
- Network/Model
- Milestones
- Precedence Diagramming Method (PDM)
- Relationships/Logic
- Resources
- Schedule update/status/progress
- Target schedules
- Work Breakdown Structure (WBS)
- Work package

Key Points for Review

❖ **Benefits of Scheduling and Why It's Important for Project Success**
❖ **Schedule Development Tools and Techniques**
  o Bar/Gantt Charts
  o Critical Path Method (CPM) / Network Models
    ✓ Arrow Diagramming Method (ADM) / i – j Node
    ✓ Precedence Diagramming Method (PDM)

  o Project Evaluation and Review Technique (PERT)/Risk Models
    ✓ Parties
    ✓ Transaction and consideration
    ✓ Written vs. oral
    ✓ Enforceability—Legal binding and interpretation

  o Overlapping Techniques
    ✓ Benefits and risks
    ✓ Relationships (predecessors and successors) (FS) (SF)
    ✓ Lags and leads (SS and FF)

❖ **Work Breakdown Structure (WBS)**
  o Defining WBS by levels and elements
  o Coding techniques
  o Activity coding

❖ **Schedule Calculations**
  o Forward pass
    ✓ Early dates (ES and EF)
    ✓ Longest path
  o Backward path
    ✓ Float
    ✓ Critical path and near critical paths
  o Work days and calendar days
  o Calculations with overlapping relationships
  o Calculations with constraints

❖ **Scheduling Levels and Reporting**
  o Levels of detail/summarization
  o Schedule reporting/communication
  o Schedule graphics/plots

❖ **Managing Schedule Change**
  o Updating for progress and change impact
    ✓ Progress update intervals
    ✓ Incorporation of change into schedule
    ✓ Forecasting
  o Reporting/communicating progress and forecasts

Check on Learning

1. The work breakdown structure (WBS) is valuable because it allows:

   A. Project details to be summarized into different groupings for analysis and control purposes
   B. All projects to be configured into the same number of work packages
   C. The highest level of the structure to represent work packages for easy reference
   D. Similar activities to have identical identifying codes

2. Activity A has a duration of five days. Activity B has a duration of 15 days and cannot start until one day after Activity A is complete. Activity C has a duration of 10 days and cannot finish until four days after Activity B is complete. The total duration of the project is:

   A. 30 days
   B. 31 days
   C. 25 days
   D. 24 days

3. Refer to question # 2. What logic change would take Activity B off of the critical path?

   A. Replace the FS relationship between Activities A and B with an SF + 21 days relationship, and replace the FF relationship between Activities B and C with an SS + 9 days relationship
   B. Remove the FS relationship between Activities A and B, and replace with an SS + 6 days relationship. Change the FF relationship between Activities B and C to FF + 0 (no lag). Create an FS + 10 days relationship between Activities A and C.
   C. Allow Activity B to start immediately after Activity A is complete and change the relationship between Activities B and C to FF + 5 days.
   D. Change the relationship between Activities A and B to FF + 16 days and the relationship between Activities B and C to SS + 9 days.

4. Refer to question # 3. What is the float of Activity B once taken off the critical path?

   A. 5 days
   B. 4 days
   C. 3 days
   D. 2 days

5. All of the following are true of a "dummy activity" except:

   A. It is unique to ADM networks
   B. It has no time duration
   C. It ensures and activity has a unique "I – j" designator
   D. It cannot be used to show relationships between activities with more than one predecessor

Use the following to answer questions 6-8.

A project consists of the following activities:

Activity	Duration	Predecessors
A	10	-
B	15	A
C	12	A (SS+5)
D	10	C
E	5	B, D

6. The project duration is:

   A. 30
   B. 32
   C. 35
   D. 37

7. The critical activities are:

   A. A, E
   B. A, B, E
   C. A, C, D, E
   D. A, B, C, D, E

8. The formula for the early start of activity E is:

   A. B, Early Finish – 1
   B. B, Early Finish + 1
   C. D, Early Finish – 1
   D. D, Early Finish + 1

9. Free Float is:

   A. Always less than total float
   B. Always more than total float
   C. Less than or equal to total float
   D. Greater than or equal to total float

10. To crash a schedule, you begin by reducing durations of the activities with:

   A. The most total float
   B. The most free float
   C. The least free float
   D. Zero total float

Solutions

1.   A   Project details to be summarized into different groupings for analysis and control purposes
    Refer to Chapter 13, "Defining Work Breakdown Structure" topic

2.   C   25 days
    Refer to Chapter 13, "Making Time Calculations" topic

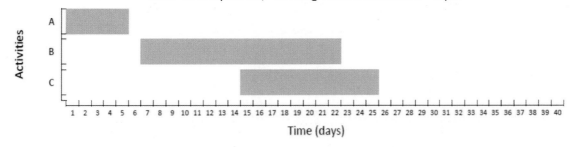

3.   B   Remove the FS relationship between Activities A and B, and replace with an SS + 6 days relationship. Change the FF relationship between Activities B and C to FF + 0 (no lag). Create an FS + 10 day relationship between Activities A and C
    Refer to Chapter 13, "The Critical Path" topic

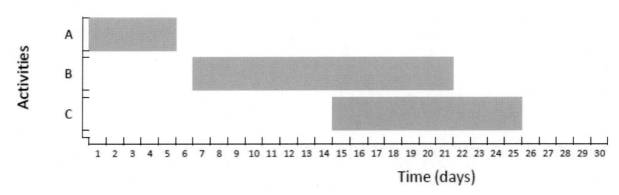

4.   B   4 days
    Refer to Chapter 13, "The Critical Path" topic

5.   D   It cannot be used to show relationships between activities with more than one predecessor
    Refer to Chapter 13, "Arrow Diagramming Method (ADM)" topic

6.   B   32
    Refer to Chapter 13, "Scheduling Techniques" topic

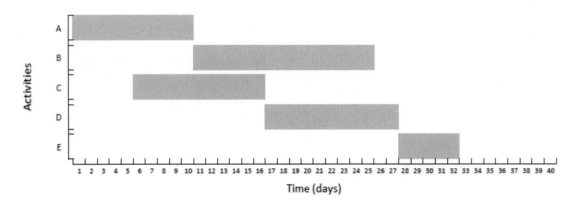

7. C   A, C, D, E
          Refer to Chapter 13, "Scheduling Techniques" topic

8. D   D, Early Finish +1
          Refer to Chapter 13, "Scheduling Techniques" topic

9. C   Less than or equal to total float
          Refer to Chapter 13, "Float" topic

10. D   Zero total float
          Refer to Chapter 13, "Float" topic

Bonus Schedule Problem #1

Draw a precedence diagram network, and calculate <u>early dates</u>, <u>late dates</u>, and <u>total float</u> for each activity based on the information in the following table:

Activity #	Description	Duration	Relationship
1	**Define Plan / Design Project**	30 days	No other activity can start until activity 1 is finished
2	**Procure, Manufacture, and Deliver Major Equipment**	60 days	Succeeds the finish of Activity 1
3	**Bids / Select Installation Contractor**	20 days	Cannot start until Activity 1 is completed
4	**Procure, Manufacture and Deliver Controls**	40 days	Starts after project design is complete
5	**Construct Equipment Foundations and Structure**	30 days	Must follow contractor selection
6	**Set Major Equipment**	10 days	Before the contractor can set major equipment, the equipment must be received and foundation and structure must be completed
7	**Install Controls**	20 days	Must occur after equipment foundations and structures are completed and controls have been delivered
8	**Start Up & Test Major Equipment**	10 days	Occurs after controls are installed and equipment is set
9	**Commission Equipment**	10 days	Starts after start up and test major equipment is complete

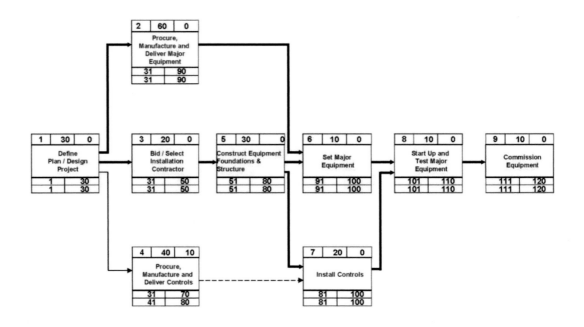

ACT	OD	TF
	DESCRIPTION	
ES		EF
LS		LF

———————— No Free Float (Driving, Non-Critical)

– – – – – – Free Float (Non-Driving)

———————— Critical Relationship

Solution for Problem #1

SECTION 4 – PROJECT AND COST CONTROL

Chapter 14 – Earned Value Overview

Sean T. Regan, CCP CEP FAACE

Introduction/Learning Objectives

This chapter reviews the current ANSI 748 Standards, as well as the commercial, international and standard U.S. government implementation and provides an understanding of the Earned Value Management System (EVMS). To learn basic earned value calculations, please refer to Chapter 19 (Project Labor Cost Control). The key learning objectives are:

- Identify the six methods used for measuring work progress.
- Understand the concept of earned value and how to use it in fixed budgets to analyze cost and schedule performance.
- Understand how to evaluate worker productivity.

Terms to Know

- Actual Cost (AC)
- Actual Cost Work Performed (ACWP)
- Budgeted Cost Work Performed (BCWP)
- Budgeted Cost Work Scheduled (BCWS)
- Cost Performance Index (CPI)
- Cost Performance Report (CPR)
- Cost Variance (CV)
- Estimate at Completion (EAC)
- Estimate to Complete (ETC)
- Integrated Baseline Review (IBR)
- Level of Effort (LOE)
- Planned Value (PV)
- Planning Package (PP)
- Project Manager (PM)
- Schedule Performance Index (SPI)
- Schedule Variance (SV)
- Statement of Work (SOW)
- Work Authorization Directive (WAD)

Key Points for Review

- ❖ **Key elements required to establish Earned Value System**
  - o Organization of Program
  - o Work Breakdown Structure (WBS)
  - o Organizational Breakdown Structure (OBS)
  - o Responsibility Assignment Matrix (RAM)
  - o Work Authorization (WA)
  - o Planning, Scheduling, and Budgeting

- Performance Measurement Baseline (PMB)
- Control Accounts (CA)
- Risk Management
- Work Package (WP)
- Planning Package (PP)
- Management Reserve and Contingency
- Earned Value Definitions
- Variance Reporting
- Change Management
- Performance Review

❖ **Earned Value Definitions**
- Planned Value – Budgeted Cost Work Scheduled (BCWS)/Planned Value (PV)
- Earned Value – Budgeted Cost Work Performed (BCWP)/Earned Value (EV)
- Milestone Value
- Physical Progress
- Incremental Phasing
- Actual Value – Actual Cost Work Performed (ACWP)/Actual Cost (AC)
- Variance Analysis
- Change Management
- Performance Reporting
- Integrated Baseline Reviews (IBR)

Check on Learning

1. The Work Authorization Document (WAD) is the "contract" of the scope, plan, and schedule between the _____ and the _____ for the project.

    A. Customer and the project manager
    B. Project manager and the control account manager (CAM)
    C. Project manager and the functional manager
    D. Customer and the control account manager (CAM)

2. The Integrated Baseline Review (IBR) process consists of the following jointly executed project management activities:

    A. PMB assessment, IBR preparation, PMB execution, management processes
    B. PMB development, IBR preparation, IBR execution, management processes
    C. PMB assessment, IBR preparation, IBR execution, management processes
    D. PMB development, IBR processes, PMB execution, management processes

3. The Performance Management Baseline (PMB) can be changed:

    A. To adjust for actual productivity
    B. In anticipation of contemplated changes
    C. By approved change orders
    D. To account for trends

4. The Performance Management Baseline (PMB) can include:

    A. Management reserve
    B. Contingency
    C. Known unknowns
    D. None of the above

5. An essential of an Earned Value System is RAM which is an acronym for:

    A. Random Access Memory
    B. Responsibility Assignment Matrix
    C. Realistic Assessment Method
    D. Reasoned Average Methodology

6. The Work Breakdown Structure is a fundamental element of an EVMS.

    A. It is a systematic approach to divide and subdivide a project's work
    B. It reflects the company's organization as integrated with a particular Project Management Office
    C. It identifies the resources associated with the control account levels established for the project
    D. It includes a list of deliverables and milestones for the project.

7. Key Characteristics of Performance Management Baseline are:

    A. Each budget is traceable to the WBS, OBS, scheduling system, and cost collection system.
    B. Budgets and schedules are established for all authorized work, at the control account level, and for undefined work at a summary level.
    C. Baseline reflects the work scope, time phased and consistent with the integrated schedule.
    D. All of the above

8. Performance reporting should occur at least on a monthly basis and NOT include:

    A. Comparison of the amount of planned budget and the amount of budget earned for work accomplished
    B. Comparison of the amount of the budget earned vs. the actual
    C. 360° Performance Reviews
    D. Differences between planned and actual schedule performance

Solutions

1.   B   The project manager is responsible for issuing the WAD, and the CAM is responsible for implementing the WAD.
> Refer to Chapter 14, "Work Authorization" topic

2.   C   An IBR is meant to be a productive assessment and evaluation of the contractor's plan to effectively and efficiently execute the project.
> Refer to Chapter 14, "Integrated Baseline Review" topic

3.   C   The Performance Management Baseline should only be changed by approved change orders.
> Refer to Chapter 14, "Performance Management Baseline" topic

4.   D   None of the above.
> Refer to Chapter 14, "Performance Management Baseline" topic

5.   B   Responsibility Assignment Matrix.
> Refer to Chapter 14, "Responsibility Assignment Matrix" topic

6.   A   It is a systematic approach to divide and subdivide a project's work.
> Refer to Chapter 14, "Work Breakdown Structure" topic

7.   D   All of the above.
> Refer to Chapter 14, "Performance Management Baseline" topic

8.   C   360° Performance Reviews
> Refer to Chapter 14, "Performance Reporting" topic

Chapter 15 – Performance and Productivity Management

Dr. James M. Neil, PE CCP FAACE AACE Hon. Life

Introduction/Learning Objectives

Companies in the business world are constantly concerned with improving efficiency, increasing their rate of return on investment, increasing the ratio of profit to revenues, or simply increasing the total profit. This goal translates into reducing worker and equipment hours per unit of output—i.e., improving productivity for production-type activities. For support and professional activities it means improving productivity. For all activities, it includes reducing waste of time, materials, and equipment. This chapter illustrates how to evaluate, analyze, and improve organization performance and productivity. The key learning objectives are:

- Analyze worker productivity and performance.
- Identify ways to increase productivity, improve performance, and minimize waste in the workplace.

Terms to Know

- Credit Workhours
- Incentive Programs
- Productivity
- Productivity Analysis
- Productivity Index
- Success Index

Key Points for Review

❖ **Success Index (SI)**
  o For a profit-oriented business

$$\text{Success index} = \frac{\text{net profit}}{\text{total cost}}$$

$$\text{Success index} = \frac{\text{net profit}}{\text{essential costs}+ \text{cost of waste}}$$

  o For a service organization (such as a government)

$$\text{Success index} = \frac{\text{value of services rendered}}{\text{costs of providing services}}$$

$$\text{Success index} = \frac{\text{value of services rendered}}{\text{essential costs}+ \text{cost of waste}}$$

❖ **Types of waste**
  o Inefficiencies inherent in the design and operation of the work place
  o Individual inefficiencies
  o Non-contributing (wasted) time by individuals
  o Waste of materials, supplies, and services (misuse, overuse, loss)

- Waste of equipment (abuse, misuse, loss)
- Functions that no longer add value to the output of the organization

❖ **Productivity Issue**

Production is dependent upon some combination of machines and personnel so both must be examined when seeking productivity improvements.

- Variability—sociological (area) factors
- Variability—location factors
- Variability—project and contract characteristics
- Variability—human factors
- Variability—field organization and management factors
- Accounting for variability in estimates
  - ✓ Range estimating
  - ✓ Checklists and worksheets
- ❖ Promoting productivity

❖ **Productivity Analysis**
- Determining percent complete—six methods for measuring and analyzing productivity
- Productivity measurement of individual work tasks
  1. Productivity $= \dfrac{\text{number of units completed}}{\text{work hours consumed}}$

- Productivity analysis at a summary level
  1. Credit work hours (CWH) = (budgeted unit rate*) x (units completed to date)
     *budgeted unit rate = budgeted hours per unit of work
  2. Productivity index $= \dfrac{\text{CWH to date}}{\text{Actual WH to date}}$
  3. For a combination of work packages or for a total project
     Productivity index $= \dfrac{\text{CWH}}{\text{actual work hours}}$

- Use of productivity data

❖ **Incentives**
- Why incentives
- The stimuli
- Rewards within the winning scenario
- Example incentive programs
- Incentive program guideline

❖ **Productivity Index Evaluation Worksheet**
- Purpose: to facilitate a comparison of the productivity potential of a proposed project with respect to a completed project
  - ✓ A productivity index of 1.0 is average
  - ✓ A productivity index less than 1.0 is less than average (unfavorable)
  - ✓ A productivity index greater than 1.0 is better than average (favorable)
- Use of worksheet—Figure 15.5

Check on Learning

1. Which of the following is not a potential constraint to Performance Expectancy?

   A. Leadership
   B. Organization
   C. Environment
   D. Union vs. Non-Union

2. Given the following variables, calculate the actual labor cost per unit work. Assume a productivity that computes <1 is below standard.

Quantity	STD Unit Rate	Productivity	Wage
100	3 WH/cy	0.8	$18/WH

   A. $43/cy
   B. $54/cy
   C. $68/cy
   D. $185/cy

3. Based on the following table:

	Dollars	Work hours	Tons	$/Ton	WH/Ton
Budget	$766,300	58,273	35,002	$21.89/T	1.66 WH/Ton
Job to date	$580,144	44,195	21,362	$27.16/T	2.07 WH/Ton
Weekly	$13,426	650	484	$27.74/T	1.34 WH/Ton

   3a. What is the budgeted dollars per work hour?

   A. $21.92
   B. $13.15
   C. $0.08
   D. $1.68

   3b. What is the job to date percent complete?

   A. 74.5 percent
   B. 75.8 percent
   C. 60.1 percent
   D. 61.0 percent

   3c. What is the job to date productivity index assuming <1 is below standard?

   A. 1.24
   B. 0.81
   C. 0.80
   D. 1.25

4. Of the 6 methods of determining percent complete which is the least accurate method?

   A. Incremental milestone
   B. Start/Finish percentages
   C. Ratio
   D. Supervisor opinion

5. Incentives are intended to stimulate employees to support management goals. Which of the following is considered the least favorable?

   A. Personal satisfaction in achieving a goal
   B. Euphoria of being singled out for recognition
   C. Career enhancement
   D. Potential loss of status, job, potential loss for promotion

6. Which of the following will not directly improve productivity performance?

   A. Earned Value Management System
   B. Waste reduction
   C. Incentive programs
   D. Reduce losses of efficiency

7. Productivity for the same work can vary from location to location. Which of the following would not be considered relevant?

   A. Sociological factors
   B. Location factors
   C. Project and contract characteristics
   D. Political party

Solutions

1.   D   Union vs. Non-Union is not a potential constraint to performance expectancy
> Refer to Chapter 15, Figure15.1

2.   C   ($18 * 3)/.8 = $68/cy
> Refer to Chapter 15, "Productivity Measurement of Individual Work Tasks" topic

3a.   B $766,300/58,273 = $13.15/WH
> Refer to Chapter 15, "Productivity Measurement of Individual Work Tasks" topic

3b.   D   21,362/35,002 = 61% complete
> Refer to Chapter 15, "Productivity Measurement of Individual Work Tasks" topic

3c.   C   1.66/2.07 = 0.8 productivity index
> Refer to Chapter 15, "Productivity Analysis at a Summary Level" topic

4.   D   Supervisor opinion
> Refer to Chapter 15, "Determining Percent Complete" topic

5.   D   Potential loss of status, job, potential loss for promotion
> Refer to Chapter 15, "The Stimuli" topic

6.   A   EVMS is necessary to evaluate productivity; but in itself, it will not directly influence productivity
> Refer to Chapter 15, "Why Incentives?" topic

7.   D   Political party
> Refer to Chapter 15, "The Productivity Issue" topic

SECTION 5 – PROJECT MANAGEMENT

Chapter 16 – Project Management Fundamentals

James E. Bent, CCP

Introduction/Learning Objectives

It is essential that the management of projects focuses on the identification of risks, cost savings, minimizing schedule delays, and an improved economic return. This chapter focuses on methods to assist in obtaining project success. The key learning objectives are:

- Understand the role of the project manager in project planning.
- Understand the major factors effecting successful project execution.
- Understand the overall company projects life cycle.
- Understand the major phases of projects.

Terms to Know

- Building Information Modeling (BIM)
- Cost Management
- Critical Path Methodology (CPM)
- Project Manager
- Project Performance Measurement (PPM)
- Time Management
- Value Engineering

Key Points for Review

❖ **Factors Essential for Successful Project Execution**
  o Identifying risks
  o Cost management (maximizing cost savings)
  o Time management (minimizing time delays)
  o Improving economic return
  o Effective management of people
  o Effective business techniques
  o Outstanding leadership skills
  o Communications

❖ **Overall Company Projects Life Cycle**
  o Engineering request
  o Project development
  o Budgeting and management
  o Project execution

❖ **Project Major Phases Flowchart**
  o Phase I—Development planning

- Phase II—Feasibility study
- Phase III—Conceptual study
- Phase IV—Project planning
- Phase V—Basic design
- Phase VI—Detail design and procurement
- Phase VII—Construction
- Phase VIII—Commission and start-up

Check on Learning

These questions and answers are related to an Engineering, Procurement, and Construction (EPC) plant project, where the total execution is the responsibility of a general or managing contractor with an owner team in a monitoring role.

1. In today's difficult and challenging business environment, what are the three major, essential elements or overall objectives? For example, "quality of engineering and construction," would be one. Which of the following is not?

    A. Identifying risks
    B. Maximizing cost savings
    C. Minimizing time delays
    D. Maximizing change orders

2. The elements or objectives listed in question 1 can only be achieved with effective people and technical processes. For example, "front-end planning," would be one such process. Which of the following is not a process?

    A. Effective management of people and challenging but achievable project objectives
    B. Comprehensive execution plan, efficient business and project control techniques, outstanding leadership skills
    C. Effective front-end planning, constructability and development of project team to fit specific project characteristics
    D. Effective management of people, efficient business and project control techniques, partnering, contracting arrangement, fast tracking

3. What is the definition of a project?

    A. It is comprised of the development of scope, in terms of risk, cost, time and resources
    B. It is comprised of major phases that may overlap
    C. A project can be loosely defined as an item of work which requires planning, organizing, dedication of resources and expenditure of funds, in order to produce a concept, a product, or a plant
    D. A project will have phases that overlap; the degree of overlap will depend on the work content of each phase and the efficiency of decision-making present in the project

4. Knowledge and experience of a typical project life cycle or individual project phases greatly enhance the capability of a project engineer in seeing the "total picture" of a project. This chapter shows there are eight phases, starting with "Development Planning" and finishing with "Commission and Start Up." Which of the following lists the other four phases?

    A. Feasibility Study Project Planning, Basic Design, Decommissioning
    B. Feasibility Study, Project Planning, Basic Design, Construction
    C. Conceptual Study, Economic Analysis Detail Design and Procurement, Construction
    D. Basic Design, Permitting, Detail Design and Procurement, Construction

5. Which of the following areas is not a project manager's constraint on a project?

   A. Resources
   B. Stakeholder
   C. Budget
   D. Scope

6. In which organization is it generally recognized that a Project Manager will have the most authority level?

   A. Balanced matrix
   B. Strong matrix
   C. Functional matrix
   D. Project manager has the same authority in all levels of the organization

7. Which of the following is aligned to a functional matrix organization?

   A. All disciplines report solely to the Project Manager
   B. Disciplines report to their respective Functional Manager
   C. Functional Managers are responsible for the program
   D. Project Manager is responsible and assigned team members work with the support of the Functional Manager

8. Which of the following is a key in the Project management communication process?

   A. Stakeholder ownership
   B. Matrix interface culture
   C. Formal and informal communication structure
   D. Project procedures

9. Which of the following is critical to the budgetary process in project management fundamentals?

   A. Scope in terms of risk, cost, time, and resources
   B. Scope in terms of risk, cost, time, and procedures
   C. Scope in terms of risk, cost, procedures, and resources
   D. Scope in terms of stakeholder, cost, time, and resources

Solutions

1.   D   Maximizing change orders
    > Refer to Chapter 16, "Key Essentials" topic

2.   D   Effective management of people, efficient business and project control techniques, partnering, contracting arrangement, and fast tracking
    > Refer to Chapter 16, "Key Essentials" topic

3.   C   A project can be defined loosely as an item of work which requires planning, organizing, dedication of resources and expenditure of funds in order to produce a concept, a product, or a plant
    > Refer to Chapter 16, "Definition of a Project" topic

4.   B   Feasibility Study, Project Planning, Basic Design, Construction
    > Refer to Chapter 16, "Typical Project Phases and Lifecycles" topic

5.   B   Stakeholder: Projects constraints are - scope, resources, quality, schedule, budget and risk
    > Refer to Chapter 16, "Cost Management, Time Management and Human Resources" topics

6.   B   In a Strong Matrix the Project Manager is the recognized authority and approval level
    > Refer to Chapter 16, "Project Management Functions" topic

7.   D   The Project Manager is responsible, but the team receives support from their functional departments for maximization of resources
    > Refer to Chapter 16, "Project Management Functions" topic

8.   C   Formal and informal process is critical in balancing the project management Fundamentals
    > Refer to Chapter 16, "Communications'" topic

9.   A   Scope in terms of risk, cost, time, and resources
    > Refer to Chapter 16, "Budgeting and Management" topic

Chapter 17 – Project Organization Structure

James E. Bent, CCP

Introduction/Learning Objectives

Project success can be achieved through effective project management. With today's market becoming more internationally based, project organizations are looking at both the matrix and functional organizations with respect to the new management theories in order to be competitive in the international market. This chapter emphasizes on project organization and planning. Key learning objectives are:

- Describe a project organization structure.
- Understand how to establish objectives.
- Define matrix structures.
- Use communication and information effectively.
- Identify a variety of contracting arrangements.
- Identify pre-contract activities for contractor evaluation.

Terms to Know

- Conflict Management
- Continuous Improvement Program (CIP)
- Equal Partner Relationship
- Matrix Organization
- Total Quality Management (TQM)

Key Points for Review

- ❖ **Background to Past Organizational Structure**
  - o Matrix structure
  - o Demingism and total quality management
    - ✓ Term "Demingism" coined after Dr. Edward Deming's approach to TQM in the 1960s and 1970s

- ❖ **Criteria for Developing a Quality Management Program**
  - o Client satisfaction
  - o Understanding and reducing variation
  - o "Top-down" management leadership and commitment
  - o Continuous change and improvement
  - o Ongoing training and education
  - o A culture of personnel pride and job satisfaction

- ❖ **Use of TQM for Effective Project Delivery**
  - o Owner qualification to perform as project manager
  - o Organization structure alignment with contracting arrangements

- o Project manager qualification
- o Determine if project manager reports to the client or to projects/engineering
- o Use of project task force (PTF)
- o Correct emphasis on business management
- o Efficient and effective project team
- o Project organization structure
- o Use of project organization charts
- o Establish authority of the project manager
- o Define project controls reporting relationship

Check on Learning

These questions and answers are related to an Engineering, Procurement & Construction (EPC) plant project, where the total execution is the responsibility of a general or managing contractor with an owner team in a monitoring role.

1. This chapter lists five major constituents for successful project execution. The first and most important is project organization. What are three of the remaining four?

    A. Establishing objectives, cost trending, scope definition control
    B. Establishing objectives, constructability planning, fast track scheduling
    C. Cost trending, fast track scheduling, communication and information use
    D. Establishing objectives, scope definition control, constructability planning

2. What are the six components of total quality management?

    A. Client satisfaction, "top-down" management leadership and commitment, performance measurement, change and improvement must be continuous, ongoing training and education is essential, a culture of personal pride and job satisfaction
    B. Client satisfaction, "top-down" management leadership and commitment, understanding and reducing variation, performance measurement, change and improvement must be continuous, a culture of personal pride and job satisfaction
    C. Client satisfaction, "top-down" management leadership and commitment, understanding and reducing variation, change and improvement must be continuous, ongoing training and education is essential, a culture of personal pride and job satisfaction.
    D. Client satisfaction, performance measurement, understand and reducing variation, change and improvement must be continuous, ongoing training and education is essential, a culture of personal pride and job satisfaction

3. What are some of the characteristics of "the Project Task Force" (PTF) approach?

    A. Used on larger projects, more efficient communication channels, challenge of bringing individuals from many parts of a company to focus on a substantial task, use of a business manager
    B. Used on smaller projects, less efficient communication channels, challenge of bringing individuals from many parts of a company is a substantial task, use of a business manager
    C. Used on larger projects, more efficient communication channels, use only individuals from one part of a company, use of a business manager
    D. None of the above

4. What is the conflict often encountered in large projects between efficiency and effectiveness of the project teams?

    A. Quality and safety
    B. Safety and cost
    C. Quality and quantity
    D. Personnel and communication

5. On cost reimbursable projects, what is the major risk an owner faces?

   A. Schedule slippage
   B. Scope creep
   C. Cost increase
   D. Quality

6. For the owner to be qualified as the project representative what would be the qualifications?

   A. Additional experience with similar projects (particularly size), having adequate in-house or consulting resources (skills and numbers), and a good project management program.
   B. Previous experience with similar projects (particularly size), having adequate in-house or consulting resources (skills and numbers), and a good project management program
   C. Owner hired independent training and consultants.
   D. Budgetary experience and management skills

7. The most effective project manager is able to assume what four roles throughout the project and has competency in each of the four areas?

   A. Leader, director, facilitator and mentor
   B. Leader, manager, director and mentor
   C. Leader, manager, facilitator and mentor
   D. Director, manager, facilitator and mentor

8. The Construction Industry Institute (CII) has identified which of the following as the most critical aspect of Project Management?

   A. Estimating
   B. Cost Control
   C. Project Planning and Organization
   D. Risk Management

9. Project Control Functions may report directly to whom?

   A. Business Manager
   B. Project Manager
   C. Construction Manager
   D. All of the above

10. An effective proposal evaluation program should evaluate the quality of the contractor's program, with individual criteria for what?

   A. Technical, project management, commercial/pricing, project control, contractual, and construction
   B. Engineering, project management, commercial/pricing, project control, contractual, and construction
   C. Technical, engineering, commercial/pricing, project control, contractual, and construction
   D. Technical, project management, engineering, project control, contractual, and construction

Solutions

1. D   Establishing objectives, scope definition control, and constructability planning.
   Refer to Chapter 17, "Introduction" topic

2. C   Client satisfaction, "top-down" management leadership and commitment, understanding and reducing variation, change and improvement must be continuous, ongoing training and education is essential, a culture of personal pride and job satisfaction.
   Refer to Chapter 17, "Demingism and Total Quality Management (TQM)" topic

3. A   Used on larger projects, more efficient communication channels, challenge of brining individuals from many parts of a company is a substantial task, use of a business manager.
   Refer to Chapter 17, "Should the Project Task Force (PTF) Approach be Used?" topic

4. C   It is the conflict of quality vs. quantity. When there is a lack of skilled personnel, "more" people of lower capability are added to compensate for this lack. This can further reduce effectiveness, especially on cost reimbursable projects where a contractor has no cost risk for adding personnel.
   Refer to Chapter 17, "Efficiency and Effectiveness of the Project Team" topic

5. C   The major risk is cost increase, resulting from or because of an "inflation" of the engineering hours and service hours.
   Refer to Chapter 17, "Project Organization Structure – Owner Team (Reimbursable Contract)" topic

6. B   Previous experience with similar projects (particularly size), having adequate in-house or consulting resources (skills and numbers), and a good project management program.
   Refer to Chapter 17, "Pre-Contract Activities for Contractor Evaluation" topic

7. C   Leader, manager, facilitator and mentor.
   Refer to Chapter 17, "is the Project Manager (The Person) Qualified?" topic

8. C   Project planning and organization are identified by CII as critical for a project.
   Refer to Chapter 17, "Introduction" topic

9. D   Project control functions generally report to either the project or business manager depending on the skill and experience level. Additionally, project controls may report to the construction manager at the job site.
   Refer to Chapter 17, "The Project Function Reports Directly to Project or Business Manager" topic

10. A   Technical, project management, commercial/pricing, project control, contractual, and construction.
    Refer to Chapter 17, "Pre-contract Activities for Contractor Evaluation" topic

Chapter 18 – Project Communications

Joseph A. Lukas, PE CCP

Introduction/Learning Objectives

This chapter explains the project communication process with a focus on the problems found in today's work environment. The importance of knowing your project stakeholders will be discussed, along with a proven method to analyze the importance and interest of the stakeholders. Elements of active listening and good listening habits will be addressed and how to read body language will be explained. Additionally, best practices for written communications will be covered along with the essential elements of a concise message. Finally, the keys to making virtual teams work will be addressed. The key learning objectives are:

- Describe the key elements of the communication process.
- Identify the filters and barriers that affect communication.
- Interpret the Stakeholder Analysis Matrix.
- Summarize the purpose of the Team Charter.
- Differentiate between positive/negative nonverbal communication clues.
- Differentiate between internal/external barriers to active listening.
- Describe the elements of the acronym **LISTEN**.
- Understand best practices for written communication.
- Describe the top five communication barriers for virtual teams.

Terms to Know

- Active listening
- Emotional intelligence
- Internal/external barriers
- Nonverbal communications
- Paralanguage
- Stakeholder
- Stakeholder Analysis Matrix
- Team Charter

Key Points for Review

❖ **Communication process**
  o Key elements of the communication process:
    ✓ Sender
    ✓ Message/transmission
    ✓ Receiver
  o Elements of the communication loop
    ✓ Sender: encodes message
    ✓ Encode:
      ▪ Symbols
      ▪ Nonverbal communication

- Paralanguage
  - ✓ Transmission: written, telephone, face-to-face
  - ✓ Receiver
  - ✓ Decode: Filters/barriers
    - Values
    - Attitudes
    - Beliefs
    - Education
  - ✓ Feedback: sent from receiver to sender

❖ **Stakeholder Analysis Matrix**
  - ○ Vertical axis: measure of power the stakeholder has over project deliverables
  - ○ Horizontal axis: measure of interest the stakeholder has regarding the project
  - ○ High interest & high power: manage closely
  - ○ High interest & low power: keep satisfied
  - ○ High power & low interest: not tied to the project but can stop the project
  - ○ Low power & low interest: require little to no attention

❖ **Team Charter**
  - ○ An agreement on operating guidelines and group behavior norms for the team
  - ○ Covers more than communications. Can include:
    - ✓ Team member roles/responsibilities
    - ✓ Administrative procedures
      - Reporting hours worked
      - Team performance measures
      - Decision-making process
    - ✓ Ground rules for team conduct
      - Dealing with issues and conflict
      - Meeting commitments
      - Returning telephone calls and emails

❖ **Nonverbal Communications**
  - ○ Four key principles:
    - ✓ Context is important
    - ✓ Observe behavior holistically
    - ✓ Watch for changes in body language
    - ✓ Watch for congruence (body language and words match)
  - ○ Positive nonverbal clues:
    - ✓ Uncrossed arms/legs
    - ✓ Open hands
    - ✓ Rubbing the chin
    - ✓ Moving closer
    - ✓ Eye contact
    - ✓ Matching (movements of speaker/listener coincide)
  - ○ Negative nonverbal clues
    - ✓ Crossed arms/legs
    - ✓ Clenched or hidden hands
    - ✓ Moving away

- ✓ Limited eye contact
- ✓ Excessive body motion

❖ **Active Listening**
- ○ Common external barriers (list not all inclusive):
  - ✓ Noise
  - ✓ Visual distractions
  - ✓ Physical setting
  - ✓ Interruptions
  - ✓ Fidgeting with objects
  - ✓ Multi-tasking
  - ✓ Speaker's personal appearance
  - ✓ Speaker's mannerisms
- ○ Common internal barriers (list not all inclusive):
  - ✓ Anxiety
  - ✓ Self-centered
  - ✓ Closed-minded/judging
  - ✓ Laziness
  - ✓ Boredom
  - ✓ Superiority
  - ✓ Preconceptions
  - ✓ Ego
- ○ Elements of **LISTEN**
  - ✓ **L**ook interested and give the speaker your undivided attention.
  - ✓ **I**nvolve yourself by responding to show you are listening.
  - ✓ **S**tay on target.
  - ✓ **T**est your understanding of what is being stated.
  - ✓ **E**valuate the message and respond appropriately.
  - ✓ **N**eutralize your feelings.

❖ **Written Communications**
- ○ Email is now the most common form of written communication
- ○ Best practices when writing and managing email:
  - ✓ Consider your audience before writing the email.
  - ✓ Use the subject line to describe email contents.
  - ✓ Keep email short, concise, and coherent.
  - ✓ Do not type in all UPPER case or all lower case.
  - ✓ Proofread your document before sending (grammar and spell check).
  - ✓ Do not attach files unnecessarily.
  - ✓ Be aware that email is not confidential.
  - ✓ Do not send emails when you are angry.

❖ **Virtual Teams**
- ○ A virtual project team is a group of geographically dispersed individuals who work across space and organizational boundaries to complete projects.
- ○ Top five communication barriers:
  - ✓ Lack of common language
  - ✓ Use of slang and terminology

- ✓ Loss of nonverbal communication clues
- ✓ Lack of team interaction
- ✓ Use of information filters
- o Achieving better virtual team communications:
  - ✓ Connect with all team members
  - ✓ Prepare e-communication plan
  - ✓ Use effective communication tools

Check on Learning

1. Which of the following is not an internal barrier to active listening?

    A. Preconceptions
    B. Visual distractions
    C. Boredom
    D. Anxiety

2. Which of the following does not affect the decoding of a message?

    A. Nonverbal clues
    B. Values
    C. Beliefs
    D. Education

3. Approximately what percentage of spoken communication of feelings and attitude is conveyed by nonverbal communication?

    A. 7%
    B. 38%
    C. 43%
    D. 55%

4. Which of the following would be considered a negative nonverbal clue?

    A. Open hands
    B. Rubbing the chin
    C. Limited eye contact
    D. Moving closer

5. How should a project manager handle a stakeholder with high interest in a project and high power over project deliverables?

    A. The stakeholder merely needs to be kept satisfied.
    B. The stakeholder should be closely managed.
    C. The stakeholder simply needs to be kept informed.
    D. The stakeholder simply needs to be monitored occasionally.

6. Which of the following is an external barrier to active listening?

   A. Self-centered
   B. Superiority
   C. Ego
   D. Speaker's personal appearance

7. There are many best practices that apply to writing and managing email. Which of the following is not one of those best practices?

   A. Considering your audience before writing an email
   B. Immediately responding to an email that upset you
   C. Proofreading your document for grammar and spelling mistakes
   D. Keeping the length of the email to less than one page

8. At a project team meeting to address rework and quality issues, you note that one of the team members states that he supports the proposed plan of action his team lead has proposed; but during the discussion you observed the team member moving his chair away from the team lead, exhibiting poor eye contact and clenching his hands. This team member is known to be a bit of an introvert. Is this team member "on board" with the proposal?

   A. Absolutely. He said he supported the proposed plan. Case closed.
   B. Absolutely. Introverts may exhibit poor eye contact and the team member said he supports the proposal.
   C. The team member may not be "on board" with the proposal. While introverts may exhibit poor eye contact, there was a lack of congruence between what was said and the body language displayed.
   D. He does support the proposal. The body and body language can lie. Verbal reactions are more reliable.

9. You have been assigned as the project manager on a project to develop a new controls system for a process modification your company is planning to make on plants they operate in five different countries on 3 continents. You have team members from all the plants and several international offices on your virtual team. The project timeline and budget do not allow for an in-person meeting so the team will be meeting virtually using drop box, video teleconferencing and e-mail. You decide to set up a team website that has a webpage which displays team member's pictures and a short paragraph that includes their educational and work background, interests and hobbies. Which of the following communication barriers are you trying to overcome?

   A. Loss of nonverbal communication clues
   B. Use of information filters
   C. Lack of team interaction
   D. Use of slang

10. You are the project manager for a 10-member team that will eventually grow to 25 members. You have been compiling your thoughts on your expectations for team communications, ground rules for team conduct and a list of the various recipients for various types of communication. What type of document have you been preparing?

    A. The project charter
    B. A stakeholder analysis matrix
    C. A project plan
    D. A team charter

Solutions

1.   B   Visual distractions (scenic window view, passerby, cluttered desk or work area) are considered an external barrier to active listening.
   > Refer to Chapter 18, "Active Listening" topic

2.   A   Nonverbal clues impact the encoding of the message but have little impact on the receiver when decoding the message.
   > Refer to Chapter 18, "The Communication Loop" topic (Figure 18.2)

3.   D   According to research conducted by Professor Albert Mehrabian, PhD, 55% of spoken communication regarding feelings and attitude is affected by nonverbal communication.
   > Refer to Chapter 18, "Communication of Feelings and Attitudes" topic (Figure 18.4)

4.   C   Negative signals indicate discomfort, distrust, and indifference. Limited eye contact is included in the list of negative nonverbal clues.
   > Refer to Chapter 18, "Body Language and Personality Styles" topic

5.   B   Stakeholders with high interest and high power should be closely managed; which may include frequent project updates and regular face-to-face meetings.
   > Refer to Chapter 18, "Know Your Stakeholders" topic

6.   D   The speaker's personal appearance is considered an external barrier to active listening.
   > Refer to Chapter 18, "Active Listening" topic

7.   B   Don't send emails when angry. A good technique is to write the email and save it as a draft until the next day.
   > Refer to Chapter 18, "Written Communication" topic

8.   C   Context is important and we need to watch for congruence when body language and words match. "Words can mislead, but the body does not lie".
   > Refer to Chapter 18, "Body Language & Personality Styles" topic

9.   C   In co-located teams, frequent team interaction can help members bond and create a positive work environment. It is harder for virtual teams to do this.
   > Refer to Chapter 18, "Virtual Teams" topic

10.   D   The team charter.
    > Refer to Chapter 18, "The Team Charter" topic

Chapter 19 – Project Labor Cost Control

Dr. Joseph J. Orczyk, PE CCP

Introduction/Learning Objectives

This chapter addresses the aspect of labor costs as a variable element of a construction project. Labor cost control is paramount to profitability for all contractors. Owners also need to control labor costs on work performed in-house and for work performed by contractors on a reimbursable basis. In order to control cost, project management must first develop a realistic budget as an inaccurate budget is useless for measuring labor cost performance. In order to maintain an accurate budget, project management must continually compare actual dollars and workhours to the budget dollars and workhours to identify deviations. Creating realistic budgets and maintaining them requires choosing an effective and efficient cost control system for controlling construction labor cost. The two prevalent construction labor cost control reporting systems are the earned value method and the unit rates method. Each method has the following elements: measuring inputs, measuring outputs, and report processing. The key learning objectives are:

- Calculate installed quantities (progress) for construction activities.
- Define how actual labor work hours are collected using time cards.
- Analyze labor cost performance using earned value.
- Analyze labor cost performance using unit rates.
- Define the three components of labor costs—quantities installed, production rates and wage rates.
- Analyze labor cost performance using variance analysis.

Terms to Know

- Actual cost of work performed (ACWP or AC)
- Budget at complete (BAC)
- Budgeted cost of work performed (BCWP or EV)
- Budgeted cost of work scheduled (BCWS or PV)
- Cost variance (CV)
- Cost performance index (CPI)
- Credit dollars
- Credit work hours
- Estimate at completion (EAC)
- Estimate to complete (ETC)
- Percent complete
- Productivity index (PI)
- Schedule performance index (SPI)
- Schedule variance (SV)
- Unit cost index

Key Points for Review

❖ **Factors Affecting Construction Craft Productivity**
  o Crew sizes and craft composition
  o Craft density (area per worker)
  o Interference with other crews
  o Scheduling
  o Material availability
  o Equipment and tool availability
  o Information availability
  o Rework as a result of design, fabrication, and field errors
  o Site layout
  o Weather
  o Constructability

❖ **Measuring Inputs and Outputs**
  o Pareto's law
  o Use of the "Rules of Credit" principle to measure outputs on tasks
  o Use of earned value method
    ✓ Percent complete calculation
    ✓ Earned value calculation
    ✓ Cost variance (CV)
    ✓ Cost performance index (CPI)
    ✓ Estimate to complete (ETC) calculation
    ✓ Credit workhours
    ✓ Unit cost index
    ✓ Productivity index
    ✓ Schedule variance
    ✓ Schedule performance index (SPI) calculation
  o The unit rate method

❖ **Analytical Techniques**
  o Two way variance analysis
    ✓ Quantity variance
    ✓ Rate variance

Check on Learning

1. What general principle applies to labor cost control?

    A. Peter Principle
    B Pareto's law
    C. Law of diminishing returns
    D. Rules of credit

2. What are the three components of Labor Cost Control?

    A. Quantities, production rate, wage rate
    B. Crew sizes, area per worker, schedule
    C. Availability of material, tools, information
    D. Rework, site layout, weather

3. Labor Cost Control is important for a project because it:

    A. Is the most visible
    B. Is the most variable
    C. Has the biggest effect on profit
    D. Deals with people not just with things

4. What term describes the project's controllable parts with respect to labor?

    A. Code of accounts
    B. Work breakdown structure (WBS)
    C. Schedule
    D. Work tasks

5. In planning and budgeting a fixed price project, a given work package was estimated to include 200 units of work. Estimators further used a unit rate of four work-hours per unit of work so they budgeted for 800 work-hours in this account. In the field, it was subsequently determined that there were really 240 units of work to be performed. This was strictly an estimating error and, with no contingency fund available, the budget remained at 800 work hours. At the end of the latest reporting period, work was 50 percent complete (120 units) and 432 work hours had been paid for. Is this package overrunning or under running cost, and is performing better or worse than planned?

    A. Overrun, worse
    B. Under run, worse
    C. Overrun, better
    D. Under run, better

6. Why such a large number of measurements are required for construction outputs?

    A. No common measure
    B. To make more work for management staff
    C. Poor up front planning

D. Reduces effect of possible errors

7. What is a cardinal rule of labor cost control?

    A. Red numbers are negative
    B. Cost of control techniques should be less than money it saves
    C. Cost is managed jointly by management, similar to the College of Cardinals
    D. If my organization is not directly at risk for labor overruns, they can be ignored

8. What factor makes accurate quantity collection on some accounts more difficult than others?

    A. Height
    B. Multiple steps
    C. Unwilling supervision
    D. Intangible quantities

9. Why should a company have a standard well-documented WBS for labor?

    A. Required for computerized cost control package
    B. Corporate control of employees
    C. Required by ISO9000
    D. Accurate cost coding of timesheets

10. What are the three basic approaches to calculating estimate at completion? Estimate at completion equals Actual + Remaining Work at which rate?

    A. Supervisor prediction, budget rate, cumulative rate to date
    B. Last period rate, cumulative rate to date, historical curves
    C. Historical curves, last period rate, budget rate
    D. Cumulative rate to date, budget rate, historical curves

11. In the earned value method, how is percent complete calculated?

    A. Management's educated guess
    B. Actual and forecasted quantities are compared
    C. Actual and budgeted hours are compared
    D. Actual and forecasted hours are compared

12. Find the ACWP, BCWP, BCWS, CWH, CPI, SPI, PI, and EAC for account data as given below. Estimate the cost of this account at completion (EAC) assuming that the cost performance to-date will continue until the end of the project. Monday through Friday are the project workdays.

    Cutoff: Friday, February 15 at 5PM
    Budget: quantity = 2000 SF; work hours = 600
    Actual: quantity = 720 SF;   work hours = 180
    Forecast total quantity = 1800 SF
    Schedule: start Wednesday, February 6; durations = 16 work days

A. 180, 240, 300, 216, 60, -60, 0.8, 450
B. 180, 216, 300, 240, 1.33, 0.8, 1.2, 540
C. 180, 240, 300, 216, 1.33, 0.8, 1.2, 450
D. 180, 240, 375, 216, 60, -60, 1.2, 450

13. Another name for BCWP is:

    A. Budgeted cost of work predicted
    B. Earned value
    C. Best calculated work prediction
    D. Credit value

14. What advantage does earned value have in an integrated project control system?

    A. Compared to unit cost
    B. Is used for estimating, thus familiar to most managers
    C. Compared to schedule percent complete
    D. Compared to value of work scheduled

15. What tool can help determine responsibility for differences between budget and estimate at completion?

    A. Regular update meetings with first level supervision
    B. Computerized cost tracking software package
    C. Two way variance analysis
    D. Polygraph

16. A manager of labor cost should concentrate on:

    A. Every level of the WBS
    B. Project level of the WBS
    C. Account level of the WBS
    D. Accounts that have negatively deviated from budget

17. You have summarized all control accounts in Area A of a project to the end of the reporting period. You note that you had scheduled 28,000 work hours, have earned 26,000 work hours, and have paid for 25,000 work hours. Analyze the cost and schedule status in Area A at the end of the reporting period by calculating SV, SPI, CV, and CPI.

    A. SV =2,000, SPI = 0.93, CV = 1,000, CPI = 1.04
    B. SV =-2,000, SPI = 1.08, CV = -1,000, CPI = 0.96
    C. SV = -2,000, SPI = 0.93, CV = 1,000, CPI = 1.04
    D. SV = 2,000, SPI = 1.08, CV = -1,000, CPI = 0.96

18. Given the data in table below, complete the worksheet from a project's status reports at the end of a reporting period. Refer to the text for the method to calculate earned value (BCWP) and percent complete for multiple accounts.

Code		U/M	Quantity Total	Quantity To-Date	Budget W/H	Earned W/H	Percent Complete
3110	Formwork	SF	5,000	5,000	5,000		
3210	Rebar	Ton	10	9	1,000		
3310	Place & Finish	CY	1,000	750	10,000		
Subtotal Slabs at Grade					16,000		
3120	Formwork	SF	5,500	550	6,000		
3220	Rebar	Ton	10	2	1,000		
3320	Place & Finish	CY	2,500	0	15,000		
Subtotal Elevated Slabs					22,000		
Total Concrete (slabs at grade plus elevated slabs)					38,000		

Solutions

1.   B   Cost control should be approached as an application of Pareto's Law, which essentially states that 80 percent of the outcome of a project is determined by only 20 percent of the included elements.
Refer to Chapter 19, "Project Labor Cost and Productivity" topic

2.   A   The three components of labor costs—quantities installed, production rates, and wage rates.
Refer to Chapter 19, "Learning Objectives" topic

3.   B   Construction labor costs are the most variable element of the project construction budget.
Refer to Chapter 19, "Introduction" topic

4.   B   A construction project is complex and must be broken into controllable parts. This is accomplished using a work breakdown structure (WBS).
Refer to Chapter 19, "Measuring inputs and outputs" topic

5.   C   Cost is 432 but 50% of budget = 400, so overrun.
Actual Unit Rate = 432/120 = 3.6 actual vs. 800/200 = 4 budget unit rate, so performance is better.
Refer to Chapter 19, "Earned Value Method" topic

6.   A   Unlike construction inputs that have the common unit of measurement (i.e., dollars and work-hours), the output cannot be measured with a common unit of measure. Consequently, a large number of measures are used for construction outputs. Examples of these measures include cubic yards of excavation, square feet of concrete formwork, tons of structural steel, lineal feet of pipe and number of electrical terminations.
Refer to Chapter 19, "Measuring inputs and outputs" topic

7.   B   A cardinal rule of cost control is that the cost of the control techniques be less than the money saved by using the cost control techniques.
Refer to Chapter 19, Labor Cost and Productivity" topic

8.   B   A major consideration for measuring construction quantities is to determine if an item (such as cubic yards of concrete placed or lineal feet of wire pulled) is installed in one step or several steps. Quantities installed in one step are the easiest to measure.
Refer to Chapter 19, "Measuring inputs and outputs" topic

9.   D   The accuracy of cost coding work-hours is improved by the following:
- Train all personnel in the use of company cost accounts to correctly code time cards.
- Check time cards for correct cost codes before recording in the cost control system.
- Develop and maintain a well-documented WBS.

Refer to Chapter 19, "Measuring inputs and outputs" topic

10.   D   Three basic approaches are provided here:
Method 1: assumes that work from this point forward will progress at the budget.
Method 2: assumes that the performance to-date will continue.
Method 3: Uses historical curves that show the normal variation.
        Refer to Chapter 19, "Earned Value Method" topic

11.   B   The percent complete for the cost account is the actual quantity divided by the forecasted total quantity (see equation 1).
        Refer to Chapter 19, "Measuring inputs and outputs" topic

12.   C   ACWP = 180
BCWP = (720/1800)*600 = 240
BCWS = (8/16)*600 = 300
CWH = (600/2000)*720 = 216
CPI = BCWP/ACWP = 240/180 = 1.33
SPI = BCWP/BCWS = 240/300 = 0.8
PI = CHW/ACWP = 216/180 = 1.2
EAC = (180/720)*1800 = 450

Wrong answer (A) CV and SV rather than CPI and SPI, and PI as actual/earned rather than earned/actual Wrong answer (B) budget rate rather than rate to-date, and BCWP and CWH transposed Wrong answer (D) = same as (a) + 7 day work week vs. 5 day
        Refer to Chapter 19, "Earned Value Method" topic

13.   B   Earned value is also referred to as the budgeted cost of work performed (BCWP).
        Refer to Chapter 19, "Measuring inputs and outputs" topic

14.   D   The earned values in the earned value method can be compared to the value of work scheduled as part of an integrated project control system.
        Refer to Chapter 19, "Conclusion" topic

15.   C   A frequent question is what or who is responsible for the total difference between the budget and the EAC? Two way variance analysis is one method for answering this question.
        Refer to Chapter 19, Two-way variance analysis" topic

16.   D   The project manager concentrates corrective efforts on those activities whose actual performance deviate from the budget. The effectiveness of the corrective action is monitored by the feedback loop.
        Refer to Chapter 19, "Conclusion" topic

17.   C   SV = 26,000-28,000 = -2,000, SPI = 26,000/28,000 = 0.93, CV = 26,000-25,000= 1,000, CPI = 26,000/25,000 = 1.04
        Refer to Chapter 19, "Earned Value Method" topic

18.

Code		U/M	Quantity Total	Quantity To-Date	Budget W/H	Earned W/H	Percent Complete
3110	Formwork	SF	5,000	5,000	5,000	5,000	100.0%
3210	Rebar	Ton	10	9	1,000	900	90.0%
3310	Place & Finish	CY	1,000	750	10,000	7,500	75.0%
Subtotal Slabs at Grade					16,000	13,400	83.8%
3120	Formwork	SF	5,500	550	6,000	600	10.0%
3220	Rebar	Ton	10	2	1,000	200	20.0%
3320	Place & Finish	CY	2,500	0	15,000	-	0.0%
Subtotal Elevated Slabs					22,000	800	3.6%
Total Concrete (slabs at grade plus elevated slabs)					38,000	14,200	37.4%

Refer to Chapter 19, "Earned Value Method" topic

Chapter 20 – Leadership and Management of Project People

Dr. Ginger Levin

Introduction/Learning Objectives

The management of human element can present more challenges to project leaders than the management of ever changing technology. This chapter examines the different approaches to leadership as discussed in detail in Chapter 20. The key learning objectives are:

- Identify the key contributors to the field.
- Understand the advantages and challenges to a multicultural team.
- Recognize the various theories of motivation.
- Identify how to avoid motivational mistakes

Terms to Know

- Culture
- Empowerment
- Ethics
- Hierarchy of needs
- Management motivation
- Motivation-hygiene theory
- Theory X management
- Theory Y management

Key Points for Review

❖ **Douglas McGregor**
- o Theory X and Theory Y Assumptions
  - ✓ Theory X control is externally imposed
  - ✓ Theory Y emphasizes self-control

❖ **Frederick Herzberg**
- o Motivation-hygiene theory
  - ✓ Satisfiers
  - ✓ Dissatisfiers

❖ **Chris Argyris**
- o Hierarchical organizational structures
  - ✓ Project teams
  - ✓ Open communication

❖ **Rensis Likert**
- o Attitude measurement/leadership styles
  - ✓ Exploitive—authoritative

- ✓ Benevolent—authoritative
- ✓ Consultative
- ✓ Participative group

- ❖ **Robert Blake and Jane Mouton**
  - o Managerial grid
    - ✓ People problems
    - ✓ Production problems

- ❖ **Effective Project Manager**
  - o Roles
    - ✓ Leader
    - ✓ Manager
    - ✓ Facilitator
    - ✓ Mentor

- ❖ **Theories of Motivation (Goal-directed behavior)**
  - o Biological perspective
  - o Drive theories
  - o Incentive theories
  - o Theory of needs
  - o Fear of failure
  - o Hierarchical theory
  - o Career stages
  - o Empowerment

Check on Learning

1. An ideal team is one that has a project manager who is knowledgeable about the technical content of the project, as well as the project management issues. An ideal team will also have members who are highly competent. In such a team, during the frequent decision making occasions, which statement best describes the Manager's action?

   A. Manager makes decisions.
   B. Manager makes decisions, encourages staff to accept those decisions.
   C. Manager obtains staff's opinions then makes decisions.
   D. Manager lets the team decide.

2. A matrixed organization has the advantage that:

   A. In the long run, it saves the company money.
   B. It allows the project to work with existing organizational structure.
   C. It gives a great degree of power to the project manager in dealing with people Issues.
   D. It makes the project team very loyal to the missions of the project.

3. When dealing with people issues in projects, managers need to be concerned about:

   A. Client people and team people.
   B. Client people, team people and those in vendor organizations.
   C. All project stakeholders.
   D. The customer organization people, client people, team people and vendor people.

4. Given that differences in opinions and backgrounds might create minor issues or major conflicts in the course of the project, the project manager must:

   A. Have a conflict management plan.
   B. Have a conflict avoidance plan.
   C. Handle minor issues and major conflicts if and when they occur.
   D. Develop a set of guidelines that encourages people avoid issues or conflicts.

5. When we compare the Theory X and Theory Y of management that describes how managers relate to their subordinates, we notice that:

   A. There is a lot of similarity between the two.
   B. They are diametrically opposite of each other.
   C. Theory X is more concerned about people than Theory Y.
   D. Theory Y works best in traditional, religious, or military organizations.

6. Which of the following is not a form of power derived from the project manager's position?

   A. Formal
   B. Reward
   C. Penalty
   D. Expert

7. From Maslow's hierarchy of needs what is the highest level listed below?

   A. Physiological satisfaction
   B. Attainment of survival
   C. The need for association
   D. Esteem

8. The halo effect is important to know because there is a tendency to:

   A. Promote from within.
   B. Hire the best.
   C. Move people into project management because they are good in their technical field.
   D. Move people into project management because they have had project management training.

9. An obstacle to team building in a matrix organization is:

   A. Team organization is technically focused.
   B. Team members are borrowed resources and can be hard to motivate.
   C. Teams are too centralized.
   D. Teams are too large to handle.

10. Which of the following conflict resolution techniques will generate the most lasting solution?

    A. Forcing
    B. Smoothing
    C. Compromise
    D. Problem solving

11. Which of the following assumptions apply to Douglas McGregor's Theory Y?
    A. The average person has an inherent dislike of work and will avoid it if possible.
    B. People are self-motivated and will exercise self-direction and self-control toward achieving objectives to which they are committed.
    C. The average person prefers to be directed, wishes to avoid responsibility, has relatively little ambition, and wants security.
    D. All of these answers are correct

12. Which of the following assumptions apply to Douglas McGregor's Theory X?

    A. The average person has an inherent dislike of work and will avoid it if possible.
    B. People are self-motivated and will exercise self-direction and self-control toward achieving objectives to which they are committed.
    C. The average person must be coerced, controlled, directed, or threatened with punishment to put forth adequate effort toward achievement of organizational objectives.
    D. All of the above

13. According to Chapter 20, which of the following are key roles that a manager must assume?

    A. Leader
    B. Facilitator
    C. Mentor
    D. All of these are roles which the manager must assume.

14. "That process, action, or intervention that serves as an incentive for a project team member to take the necessary action to complete a task within the appropriate confines and scope of performance, time, and cost", according to Chapter 20, is the definition of:

    A. Leadership
    B. Motivation
    C. Actual authority
    D. Implied authority

Solutions

1.   D   Manager lets the team decide
   Refer to Chapter 20, "Teams & Cross-Cultural Concerns" topic

2.   B   It allows the project to work with existing organizational structure
   Refer to Chapter 20, "Concepts" topic

3.   C   All project stakeholders
   Refer to Chapter 20, "Leading, Managing, Facilitating, and Mentoring" topic

4.   A   Have a conflict management plan
   Refer to Chapter 20, "Facilitation, Ethical Theories and Applications" topic

5.   B   They are diametrically opposite of each other
   Refer to Chapter 20, "Concepts" topic

6.   D   Expert
   Refer to Chapter 20, "Leading, Managing, Facilitating, and Mentoring" topic

7.   D   Esteem
   Refer to Chapter 20, "Theories of Motivation" topic

8.   C   Move people into project management because they are good in their technical field
   Refer to Chapter 20, "Theories of Motivation" topic

9.   B   Team members are borrowed resources and can be hard to motivate.
   Refer to Chapter 20, "Teams & Concepts" topic

10.   D   Problem solving
    Refer to Chapter 20, "Facilitation, Ethical Theories & Applications" topic

11.   B   People are self-motivated and will exercise self-direction and self-control toward achieving objectives to which they are committed.
    Refer to Chapter 20, "Douglas McGregor" topic

12.   A   The average person has an inherent dislike of work and will avoid it if possible
    Refer to Chapter 20, "Douglas McGregor" topic

13.   D   The manager must assume as leader; facilitator and mentor
    Refer to Chapter 20, "Leading, Managing, Facilitating and Mentoring" topic

14.   B   Motivation
    Refer to Chapter 20, "What is Motivation?" topic

Chapter 21 – Quality Management

Gary Cokins

Introduction/Learning Objectives

This chapter introduces quality management concepts and other current concepts such as Six Sigma, as well as their implications for cost professionals. Quality management is one of a suite of management tools essential for producing a quality product meeting the expectation of all parties. The key learning objectives are:

- Understand a brief history of the quality management, continuous improvement, and benchmarking movements.
- Appreciate why there is renewed interest in quality management, now emerging as the convergence of lean management and Six Sigma.
- Understand why traditional managerial accounting has failed the quality management movement.
- Understand the Cost of Quality (COQ) categories: error-free, conformance related, and non-conformance related.
- Understand how Activity Based Cost Management (ABC/M) provides a foundation for repetitively and reliably computing COQ.
- Appreciate the goals and uses of COQ and benchmarking data.

Terms to Know

- Activity Based Cost Management (ABC/M)
- Activity Value
- Benefit Cost Analysis
- Cost of Quality (COQ)
- Cost of Quality Conformance
- Cost of Quality Non-Conformance
- Quality Performance Tracking System
- Total Quality Management (TQM)

Key Points for Review

- ❖ History and renewed emphasis on quality management
- ❖ Evolution of value realization
- ❖ Equation for value:
  - o Value = Performance/Cost
- ❖ Pitfalls of applying traditional accounting to quality management
- ❖ Goals of quality management
  - o Lower costs
  - o Higher revenues
  - o Delighted customers
  - o Empowered employees

- ❖ Categorizing quality costs
  - o Error-free costs
  - o Cost of Quality (COQ)
    - ✓ Costs of conformance
      - ▪ Prevention
      - ▪ Appraisal
    - ✓ Costs of non-conformance
      - ▪ Internal failure
      - ▪ External failure
  - o Hidden poor quality costs
    - ✓ Postponed profits
    - ✓ Lost profits
    - ✓ Customer incurred costs
    - ✓ Socio-economic costs
- ❖ Improving profits by reducing error-free costs and COQ
- ❖ ABC/M assigns 100% of the resource costs to 100% activities and enables driving down quality costs
- ❖ Cost-of-quality components

Check on Learning

1. Which are the major accredited quality management programs?

    A. The Malcolm Baldrige National Quality Award and the European Quality Award
    B. The American Society for Quality's King Quality Award
    C. The American Institute of CPAs Cost of Quality Award
    D. The American Production and Inventory Control Society (APICS) Award for Class A TQM

2. When the costs of business processes and their outputs (e.g., product costs) can be adequately measured financially, what can then be enabled?

    A. Accountability can be targeted to remove underperforming employees and managers
    B. Six Sigma programs can then be initiated
    C. Quality teams can challenge their organization's pricing of their products and service customers
    D. Management's confidence can be gained so that it can depend on the managerial accounting system for decision support

3. What has research documented as the two main reasons that most organizations do not measure and track their cost of quality (COQ)?

    A. Insufficient budget and resources
    B. Lack of management interest and the belief that the "paperwork" to do it does not have enough value
    C. The accounting general ledger code structure would require changing and new input forms would be required
    D. Most quality professional do not want to be held accountable for their performance and the belief that another department is the main source for their department's quality problems

4. Other than the "error-free" costs of first-time-correct processing costs, what are the two broad sub-categories of the "cost of quality" (COQ)?

    A. Prevention costs and failure-related costs
    B. Costs of conformance and nonconformance
    C. Incurred costs and opportunity costs
    D. Quality department costs and hidden non-quality department costs

5. How does an activity-based cost management (ABC/M) system resolve perceived issues with measuring and reporting COQ on a repeatable basis?

    A. It removes the accounting department from having any say or influence with the quality function's interests
    B. It requires hand-held data collection scanning devices to assure precision and detail—key requirements of a cost accounting system
    C. It sparks debate and controversy that are useful for quality problem identification and correction
    D. It transforms the structurally-deficient coding scheme of a the general ledger accounting

system into a "chart of work activities" and then tags each type of work with an "attribute" cross-referenced to the organization's cost of quality classifications

6. To improve organization efficiency and increase profits, corporation executives are more likely to implement:

    A. Total Quality Management
    B. Lean management
    C. Customer relationship management
    D. All of the above

7. Which one of the following is not related to the supply chain-related hidden quality costs?

    A. Postponed profits
    B. Customer incurred costs
    C. Error-free costs
    D. Socio-economic costs

8. Which one of the following is not related to the cost of quality (COQ)?

    A. Costs of prevention programs
    B. Lost profits
    C. Costs of internal failure
    D. Costs of appraisal programs

9. The rationale for implementing COQ measurement system is based on the following logic:

    A. For any failure, there is a root cause
    B. Causes for failure are preventable
    C. Prevention is cheaper than fixing problems after they occur
    D. All of the above

10. Which one of the following components is not related to the cost of quality due to internal failure?

    A. Warranty expenses
    B. Rework
    C. Lost process time
    D. Scrap

Solutions

1.   A   Malcolm Baldrige National Quality Award and the European Quality Award
   > Refer to Chapter 21, "Renewed emphasis on quality management" topic

2.   D   Management's confidence can be gained so that it can depend on the managerial accounting system for decision support.
   > Refer to Chapter 21, "Why is traditional accounting failing quality management?" topic

3.   B   Lack of management interest and the belief that the "paperwork" to do it does not have enough value.
   > Refer to Chapter 21, "Categorizing quality costs" topic

4.   B   Costs of conformance and nonconformance are sub-categories of the "cost of quality".
   > Refer to Chapter 21, "Categorizing quality costs" topic

5.   D   It transforms the structurally-deficient coding scheme of a the general ledger accounting system into a "chart of work activities" and then tags each type of work with an "attribute" cross-referenced to the organization's cost of quality classifications.
   > Refer to Chapter 21, "Categorizing quality costs" topic & Fig. 21.5

6.   D   Implement total quality management, lean management, and customer relationship management to improve organization efficiency and increase profits
   > Refer to Chapter 21, "Renewed emphasis on quality management" topic

7.   C   Error-free costs are not part of the supply chain-related hidden quality costs
   > Refer to Chapter 21, "Categorizing quality costs" topic

8.   B   Lost profits are not related to the cost of quality
   > Refer to Chapter 21, "Categorizing quality costs" topic

9.   D   The rationale for implementing COQ measurement system is based all failures have root causes; all failures are preventable and it is more cost effective to prevent failure from happening
   > Refer to Chapter 21, "Categorizing quality costs" topic

10.   A   Warranty expenses are not related to the cost of quality due to internal failure
    > Refer to Chapter 21, "Decomposing Cost-of-Quality categories" topic & Fig. 21.9

Chapter 22 – Value Engineering

Neil D. Opfer, CCP CEP PSP FAACE

Introduction/Learning Objectives

The objective of this chapter is to present the key concepts involved in value engineering (VE) and the VE job process. The key learning objectives are:

- Express a more detailed understanding of value management.
- Identify the detailed steps of the value management process.
- Conduct a value management workshop.
- Conduct a value management review process.
- Identify the practical steps for implementation of the value management process.
- Understand value management implementation and its impact on the budget and schedule.

Terms to Know

- FAST (Function Analysis Systems Technique) Diagram
- Law of Unintended Consequences
- Level of Influence Curve
- Pareto's Law of Optimality
- The "80-20" Rule
- Value Engineering (VE)
- Value Engineering Job
- Value Engineering Success Steps
- Value Types

Key Points for Review

❖ **Factors causing poor value**
  o Poor attitudes
  o Poor habits
  o Poor ideas
  o Poor information
  o Time constraints
  o Temporary circumstances
  o Mistaken beliefs

❖ **Value types include**
  o Cost value
  o Exchange value
  o Use value
  o Esteem value

❖ **Level of influence curve**
  o Engineering/design – High influence on costs with low expenditure
  o Procure/construct – Low influence with high expenditure

❖ **Project schedule**
  ○ Optimum project duration results in the lowest life cycle cost

❖ **Functional Analysis Systems Technique (FAST)/Functional Approach**
  ○ Identify unnecessary costs
  ○ Use an active verb and measurable noun
  ○ Identify primary functions and secondary functions
  ○ Use "Why" and "How" to stimulate thinking

❖ **Value Engineering study team**
  ○ Diversified team members
  ○ Variety of relevant specializations

❖ **Value Engineering job plan**
  ○ Information Phase
  ○ Speculation Phase
  ○ Analysis Phase
  ○ Development Phase
  ○ Presentation Phase
  ○ Follow-up and Implementation Phase

❖ **Value Engineering success steps**
  ○ An organized creative approach to cost reduction
  ○ Targets function versus technique
  ○ Targets areas of unneeded costs
  ○ Enhance the value of the product or service
  ○ Same level, or improved performance level, at reduced cost
  ○ Does not harm quality or reliability

Check on Learning

1. The four types of value in value engineering include all of the following EXCEPT:

    A. Use value
    B. Exchange value
    C. Cost value
    D. Opportunity value

2. In the stages of value engineering, the stage where numerous alternatives are developed is termed as the _____.

    A. Information phase
    B. Speculative phase
    C. Analytical phase
    D. Proposal phase

3. In value engineering, what key purpose does the FAST diagram have?

    A. Diagram cost savings
    B. Eliminate unnecessary functions
    C. Diagram functions
    D. Identify effectively unnecessary costs

4. Approximately for how long have the value engineering techniques been around?

    A. 10 years
    B. 30 years
    C. 60 years
    D. 90 years

5. What does the acronym FAST stand for?

    A. Functional Analysis Systems Technique
    B. Fair Analysis Synergistic Technique
    C. Forcible Amplification Soundness Technique
    D. Functional Amplification Separation Technique

6. The key lesson that the "level of influence" curve teaches is that:

    A. Value engineering efforts can be most effectively applied at the operations stage of a product, project or service
    B. Value engineering efforts can be most effectively applied at the production/construction stage of a product, project or service
    C. Value engineering efforts can be most effectively applied at the completion of the design stage of a product, project or service
    D. Value engineering efforts can be most effectively applied at the engineering/design stages of a product, project or service

7. Pareto's Law of Optimality is also known as the:

    A. "60-40" Rule
    B. "50-50" Rule
    C. "20-80" Rule
    D. "80-20" Rule

8. In value engineering, the key metric upon which value engineering success is measured is the:

    A. Analysis phase
    B. Development phase
    C. Presentation phase
    D. Follow-up/implementation phase

9. Which one of the following best describes the cause of poor value?

    A. Poor information
    B. Time constraints
    C. Temporary circumstances
    D. All of the above are reasons

10. Organizations implementing value engineering have seen returns on the value engineering investment (VE team member's VE time, implementation costs) often in the range of _____.

    A. 25%
    B. 100%
    C. 200%
    D. 300%

Solutions

1.   D   Opportunity value. The four types of value are use value, esteem value, cost value and exchange value.
Refer to Chapter 22, "Value Types" topic

2.   D   Speculative phase
Refer to Chapter 22, "Phase Two – Speculative Phase" topic

3.   D   Identify effectively unnecessary costs.
Refer to Chapter 22, "FAST Diagram/Functional Approach" topic

4.   C   60 years. Value engineering techniques came about during World War II.
Refer to Chapter 22, "Introduction" topic

5.   A   Functional Analysis Systems Technique.
Refer to Chapter 22, "FAST Diagram/Functional Approach" topic

6.   D   Value engineering efforts can be most effectively applied at the engineering/design stages of a product or service (Review the Level of Influence Curve through its three distinct phases and the labels on the Curve).
Refer to Chapter 22, "Level of Influence Curve" topic

7.   D   "80-20" Rule. Pareto's Law of Optimality also known as the "80-20" Rule states that 80% of the cost of an item is in only 20% of the components of that item.
Refer to Chapter 22, "FAST Diagram/Functional Approach" topic

8.   D   Follow-up/implementation phase. The key measure or metric of success in value engineering is what percentage/cost impact of recommendations that were proposed in VE actually receives final implementation.
Refer to Chapter 22, "The Value Engineering Job Plan" topic

9.   D   All of the above are causes for poor value.
Refer to Chapter 22, "Why Is There Poor Value" topic

10.   D   300%.
Refer to Chapter 22, "Value Engineering Benefits" topic

Chapter 23 – Contracting For Capital Projects

James G. Zack, Jr., CFCC FAACE AACE Hon. Life

Introduction/Learning Objectives

This chapter defines the elements that make up a valid contract and the various contracting arrangements common in capital projects, and demonstrates why understanding the fundamental elements of contracting, is a key to good cost and schedule management. The key learning objectives are:

- Understand the basic requirements of a contract.
- Understand how contracts may become defective and possibly, unenforceable.
- Understand the types of contracts typically employed in capital projects, their requirements and the potential advantages and disadvantages of each.
- Understand typical project delivery methods and how contracts are employed in each method.
- Understand various key clauses in contracts.

Terms to Know

- Contract
- Mistakes
- Risk

Key Points for Review

- ❖ **Contract Elements**
  - o Details definition of a contract
    - ✓ Offer
    - ✓ Acceptance
    - ✓ Legality of purpose
    - ✓ Competent parties
    - ✓ Consideration

- ❖ **Mistakes that Make Contracts Defective**
  - o Nature of the transaction
  - o Identity of a party
  - o Identity of the subject matter
  - o Existence of the subject matter

- ❖ **Mistakes that <u>Do Not</u> Make Contracts Defective**
  - o Value, quality or price
  - o Terms of the contract

- ❖ **Other Factors Affecting Enforceability of Contracts**
  - ○ Statutory or regulatory provisions
    - ✓ Valid contractor's license
    - ✓ Valid professional engineering or land survey registration

- ❖ **Parties to a Contract**
  - ○ Owner
  - ○ Contractor
  - ○ Related parties
  - ○ Third parties

- ❖ **Written Contract Issues**
  - ○ Why in writing?
  - ○ Set forth the duties, obligations, and responsibilities of the parties involved
  - ○ Define the commercial terms and conditions
  - ○ Changes/modifications
  - ○ Notice and documentation

- ❖ **Contents of a Contract**
  - ○ Contract elements (terms and conditions)
  - ○ Reference documents included in a contract
  - ○ Scope of work
  - ○ Change Orders or Contract Modifications
  - ○ Uniform Commercial Code

- ❖ **Types of Contracts**
  - ○ Fixed price – lump sum contracts
    - ✓ With economic adjustment
    - ✓ With incentives
  - ○ Fixed price – unit price contracts
  - ○ Cost reimbursable contracts
    - ✓ Direct cost considerations
    - ✓ Indirect cost considerations
    - ✓ Mark up cost consideration
  - ○ Target or guaranteed maximum price (GMP) contracts

- ❖ **Why Use a Particular Form of Contract?**
  - ○ Project delivery methods
  - ○ Requirement
  - ○ Advantages
  - ○ Disadvantages
  - ○ Risks and mitigations
    - ✓ Contractor prequalification
    - ✓ Bid/no bid decisions
    - ✓ Mitigation measures

❖ **Key Contract Clauses**
  o Audit
  o Changes
  o Contractor Responsibilities
  o Delays
  o Differing Site/Changed Conditions
  o Dispute Resolution
  o Force Majeure
  o Governing Law
  o Indemnification
  o Insurance
  o Late Completion Damages
  o Limitation of Liability
  o No Damages for Delay
  o Order of Precedence
  o Owner Responsibilities
  o Payments
  o Quantity Variations
  o Schedules
  o Suspension of Work
  o Termination
  o Time of the Essence/Time of Performance
  o Warranty

Check on Learning

1. What is the difference between an agreement and a contract?

    A. The element of legal enforceability
    B. There is no difference
    C. One is for social transactions and the other for business transactions
    D. One requires a meeting of the minds and the other does not

2. A mistake that will make a contract defective and unenforceable is a

    A. Mutual mistake as to the nature of the transaction
    B. Mistake as to cost of the work to be performed
    C. Mistake concerning the terms of the contract
    D. Mistake as to the quality requirement of the work

3. A Lump Sum contract places most of the risk on

    A. The owner
    B. The design professional
    C. The contactor
    D. The drafter of the contract

4. Fixed Price contracts with Economic Price Adjustment clauses

    A. Allow subcontractors and vendors to adjust their prices after contract award
    B. Allow the owner to change the contract's pricing mechanism
    C. Provide the construction manager the right to reprice the Schedule of Values at any time
    D. Entitle the contractor to seek price adjustments of named items when costs increase or decrease by a stipulated percentage

5. One disadvantage of a Unit Price contract is

    A. Good design definition is required
    B. Not very suitable for competitive bidding
    C. Unit price contracts are not very flexible concerning changes
    D. Final cost is not known until the project is fully constructed

6. An advantage of a Cost Reimbursable contract is …

    A. Total project cost is established at the time of contract execution
    B. Contractor is incentivized to complete work early and under budget
    C. Contractor is assigned almost all risk under the contract
    D. Contract is very flexible concerning changes during performance

7. Under a design/build contract…

    A. Design must be complete prior to start of construction

B. Owner is not at risk for coordination between the designer and the contractor
C. Design and construction must still be procured competitively and separately
D. Total project cost is known at the time of contract execution

8. Under a multiple prime contract arrangement...

    A. Prime contracts may only be let by trade and craft in accordance with State contracting license statutes
    B. Entire project must be designed prior to bidding the prime contracts
    C. Owner still retains the design professional directly as the single point of responsibility for planning and design
    D. Owner's risk of claims from each prime contractor is reduced

9. A Differing Site Condition clause...

    A. Assigns all risk of site conditions to the contractor
    B. Is intended to alert the contractor to allocation of risk for site conditions so they can include an appropriate amount of contingency in their bid
    C. Assigns all risk of latent physical conditions at the site to the owner
    D. In unenforceable in many States

10. Liquidated damages in a contract...

    A. Are a penalty in the event the contractor completes the project later than planned
    B. Must reflect actual damages in order to be enforceable
    C. Are an estimate of damages the owner is likely to incur if the project is completed late
    D. Must be proven by the owner before they can be assessed to the contractor

Solutions

1. A   A contract is legally enforceable, whereas an agreement is not.
    Refer to Chapter 23, "Definition of a Contract" topic

2. A   If there is no agreement concerning the nature of the transaction or the scope of work to be performed, then the contract is defective and unenforceable.
    Refer to Chapter 23, "Mistakes as to the Nature of the Transaction" topic

3. C   A Lump Sum contract places most of the risk of contract time and price on the contractor.
    Refer to Chapter 23, "Fixed Price – Lump Sum Contracts" topic and Figures 23.1 & 23.2

4. D   Contracts with Economic Price Adjustment clauses allow the contractor to seek a price adjustment for specified items identified in the contract should the cost of these items increase or decrease more than a stipulated percentage.
    Refer to Chapter 23, "Fixed Price with Economic Adjustment" topic

5. D   On a Unit Price contract the value of the contract is unknown until the end of the project when all units have been put in place and the owner can calculate the actual units installed.
    Refer to Chapter 23, "Fixed Price – Unit Price Contracts" topic and Figures 23.1 & 23.2

6. D   One substantial advantage to a Cost Reimbursable contract is that the contract is quite flexible with respect to changes during performance as cost need not be negotiated in advance of making a change to the contract as the contractor will recover the costs expended.
    Refer to Chapter 23, "Cost Reimbursable Contracts" topic and Figures 23.1 & 23.2

7. B   Since the Design-Build organization is responsible for both design and construction, the owner has little to no risk for coordinating between the design team and the construction team; as they both belong to a single organization.
    Refer to Chapter 23, "Design-Build Project Delivery Method" topic

8. C   Under the Multiple Prime project delivery method, the project owner still retains the services of the design professional directly and provides the design documents to each of the independent prime contractors.
    Refer to Chapter 23, "Multiple Prime Contract Project Delivery method" and Figure 23.7

9. C   The purpose of the Differing Site Condition clause is to transfer the risk of latent site conditions to the project owner in order to entice bidders to reduce their bid contingency. Thus, the owner is left to pay only for unexpected conditions encountered during performance of the work.
    Refer to Chapter 23, "Differing Site Conditions or Changed Conditions" topic

10.   C   Liquidated Damages are a pre-agreed cost per day for every day of late completion which is not excusable to the contractor. The Liquidated Damages amount in the contract must be based upon a reasonable estimate of the damages the owner is likely to incur should the project work not be completed on time.
           Refer to Chapter 23, "Late Completion Damages" topic

Chapter 24 – Strategic Asset Management

John K. Hollmann PE CCP CEP DRMP FAACE AACE Hon. Life

Introduction/Learning Objectives

The objective of this chapter is to show how the skills and knowledge of cost engineering work from an asset owner's perspective (as opposed to a project team perspective). For the asset owner, the concepts, tools, and resources of cost engineering are applied in an integrated way through the strategic asset management — a sub-process of Total Cost Management (TCM).This chapter describes Strategic Asset Management and provides examples of how it works in practice. The key learning objectives are:

- Understand how cost engineering practices can be applied in an integrated way using the Strategic Asset Management process.
- Understand how Strategic Asset Management is applied in different industries and for different asset types.
- Understand typical roles and responsibilities of cost engineers in Strategic Asset Management.

Terms to Know

- Asset Life Cycle
- Benchmarking
- Capital Asset
- Capital Budget
- Economic Life Cycle
- Enterprise
- Enterprise Resource Planning (ERP)
- Front-End Loading (FEL)
- Influence Curve
- Product Life Cycle
- Project Life Cycle
- Project System
- Project System, Gated (Also, Stages and Gates Project System)
- Strategic Asset
- Strategic Asset Management
- Total Cost Management (TCM)
- Value Improving Practice (VIP)

Key Points for Review

- ❖ **TCM and Strategic Asset Management**
  - o The AACE International *Total Cost Management Framework* defines TCM as the sum of the practices and processes that an enterprise uses to manage the total life cycle cost investment in its portfolio of strategic assets
  - o Strategic asset
    - ✓ Physical property: Industrial plants; transportation systems

- ✓ Intellectual property: software programs
  - o Strategic asset management
    - ✓ Strategic asset planning
    - ✓ Strategic asset (project) implementation
      - Project planning
      - Project control plan implementation
      - Project performance measurement
      - Project performance assessment
    - ✓ Strategic asset performance measurement
    - ✓ Strategic asset performance assessment
    - ✓ Strategic Asset Management and Project Control sub-processes are linked in TCM

❖ Asset and Project System Performance Measurement
  - o Asset performance measurement
    - ✓ Safety
    - ✓ Cost
    - ✓ Quality
    - ✓ Operational efficiency
    - ✓ Resource consumption (e.g., materials, labor, energy, etc.)
  - o Project system performance measurement
    - ✓ Safety
    - ✓ Cost
    - ✓ Quality
    - ✓ Schedule

❖ Asset Planning
  - o Owner identifies asset investment and Project System options, defines and evaluates them, and decides upon which options to move.
    - ✓ Investment options identification step, finds ways to improve asset or Project System performance.

❖ Implementation
  - o Based upon the decision process to implement an asset or Project System improvement idea
    - ✓ Planning focus on developing the technical scope and execution plans
    - ✓ Formal documentation inclusive of budget and operating cost should be added to the capital budget
    - ✓ During implementation, the asset is reviewed continually on its technical scope and execution plan
    - ✓ Project definition is also known as the front-end loading (FEL) phase
    - ✓ With good FEL, late changes in scope are minimal
    - ✓ At completion of FEL, project has a detailed budget and schedule that serve as the basis for project control during execution

❖ Application—Capital or Fixed Assets
  - o Includes items such as manufacturing plants and equipment, buildings, roads, utilities, and similar items that are not easily moved and have significant-useful lifespans
    - ✓ Generally created, modified and retired through a project process
    - ✓ List of opportunities and challenges identified by strategic planning is long

- ✓ Review improving technology against plans, basis and assumptions
- ✓ Process application is reviewed against estimating, historical data, schedule, risk, value engineering and then results in the decision analysis
- ✓ Documentation and decision analysis are key to the process

❖ **Application—Products**
  - o Include such as items as manufactured goods and similar items that have a limited useful lifespan
    - ✓ Products are created through an ongoing, discrete or continuous manufacturing or production process, rather than a project process
    - ✓ Teams should develop a flow chart of business operations that reviews flow of all backgrounds
    - ✓ Process for products is similar to capital planning

❖ **Application—Software**
  - o Difficult to classify software as either a capital asset or product
    - ✓ May or may not have a limited-useful lifespan
    - ✓ May not be fixed depending on installation in a particular device
    - ✓ Software estimates deal with configuration and coding activities versus construction or actual assemblies

Check on Learning

1. Which answer best describes the "stages (or phases) and gates" project system?

    A. A system for developing a project schedule
    B. A system for planning or developing project scope definition
    C. A system for training and development of project personnel
    D. A system for tracking project physical progress

2. Which answer best describes the principle behind an "influence curve" chart?

    A. The influence on profitability of payments or revenues as time progresses
    B. The ability to influence project value as project planning progresses
    C. The influence personnel have on project performance depending on their level in an organization chart
    D. The influence personnel have on project performance depending on their productivity

3. Which answer best describes the concept of "front-end loading (FEL)" in relation to project scope?

    A. Achieving a more definitive level of project planning before a project is approved
    B. Defining the scope of early activities in a project schedule before later ones
    C. Addressing priority concerns first in a project status review meeting
    D. Approving funding for a project earlier in its life cycle

4. According to total cost management (TCM), which best describes the differences between the "strategic asset management" and "project control" processes?

    A. Strategic asset management deals with cost engineering/cost management during the asset life cycle and project control during the project life cycle
    B. Project control is focused on "cost control" while strategic asset management is focused on "cost management"
    C. The strategic asset management process is focused on the cost management "big picture" rather than details such as in the project control process
    D. The strategic asset management process can be done successfully without a project control process, but not vice-versa

5. Which best describes the primary long-term benefit of "benchmarking" to an enterprise during strategic asset management?

    A. Supports performance improvement by identifying best practices and performance of others
    B. Provides important marketing information for advertising an enterprise's product benefits versus its competitor's
    C. Reduces uncertainty as to the performance of an asset investment by comparing it to the performance of other assets
    D. Provides more leverage in negotiations by identifying the negotiating positions of other enterprises

6. In Strategic Asset Management, tangible assets would be considered as all of the following except:

    A. Plant buildings
    B. Equipment
    C. Patents
    D. Process control system

7. The PDCA Cycle is an acronym for what?
    A. Plan, Develop, Check, Act
    B. Plan, Develop, Check, Assess
    C. Plan, Do, Check, Act
    D. Plan, Do, Control, Act

8. Concerning the Influence Curve, the segment that has the highest potential to influence value is:

    A. Asset Planning (Business FEL)
    B. Asset Implementation (Project FEL)
    C. Project Control
    D. Project Close-out

9. A measurement and analysis process that compares the firm's practices and processes, etc. to that of peer organizations within the same industry or across other industries is commonly referred to as:

    A. Performance Measurement
    B. Total Cost Management
    C. Benchmarking
    D. Value Improving Practice

10. In most large organizations, _____ is a key interface point between cost engineering and the accounting/finance groups.

    A. FEL
    B. ERP
    C. TCM
    D. SAM

Solutions

1.   B   A system for planning or developing project scope definition
   > Refer to Chapter 24, "TCM and Strategic Asset Management" topic

2.   B   The ability to influence project value as project planning progresses
   > Refer to Chapter 24, "Implementation" topic

3.   A   Achieving a more definitive level of project planning before a project is approved
   > Refer to Chapter 24, "Implementation" topic

4.   A   Strategic asset management deals with cost engineering/cost management during the asset life cycle and project control during the project life cycle
   > Refer to Chapter 24, "TCM and Strategic Asset Management" topic

5.   A   Supports performance improvement by identifying best practices and performance of others
   > Refer to Chapter 24, "Asset Performance Assessment" topic

6.   C   Patents are considered intangible property. Answer "D" would be incorrect since the process control system could represent both tangible and intangible property such as the hard wiring/processers (tangible) and potential intellectual property (intangible).
   > Refer to Chapter 24, "Strategic Assets" and Chapter 10, "Amortization" topics

7.   C   Plan, Do, Check, Act
   > Refer to Chapter 24, Figure 24.1: Total Cost Management Process Map topic

8.   A   Asset Planning (Business FEL)
   > Refer to Chapter 24, "Influence Curve" topic and Figure 24.3 wherein on the "Y" axis this segment has the highest impact on influencing value.

9.   C   Benchmarking is the best answer.
   > Refer to Chapter 24, "Asset Performance Assessment" topic

10.   B   ERP or Enterprise Resource Planning.
    > Refer to Chapter 24, "Asset and Project System Performance Measurement" topic

DISCUSSION CASES

I.   Consider an enterprise that has significant capital assets, but no one trained in the skills and knowledge of cost engineering to support asset management. Discuss how asset management at such an enterprise might be less effective than otherwise.

II. Consider the case of the strategic assets that are owned by an enterprise that you are familiar with (company, department, school, church, home, etc.). Discuss how an integrated strategic asset management process might apply in that situation.

III. Consider the case of a contractor cost engineer working on a project (e.g., project control, estimating, etc.). Discuss how having an understanding of the client owner's asset management process might help that cost engineer be a more valuable contributor to successful project execution.

IV. Consider an asset implementation decision (e.g., build a building, create a software program, etc.) that you are familiar with that either did or did not meet its objectives. Discuss the reason that it was or was not successful and whether an integrated asset management process that applied cost engineering skills and knowledge would have or did make a difference in its success.

Chapter 25 – Change Management Practical Guide

Sean T. Regan, CCP CEP FAACE

Introduction/Learning Objectives

Change Management is the process of identifying, resolving, reporting, and administering changes to a project that affects its scope, cost, or schedule. Change Management and Control has proven to be an essential part of controlling a project and it is critical for the project team's ability to successfully manage the work effort. The key learning objectives are:

- Understand basic change management concepts.
- Identify steps in the change management process.
- Conduct a change management review process.
- Implement practical steps in the change management process.
- Understand change management implementation and its impact on the budget and schedule.

Terms to Know

- Change Order
- Change Procedure
- Change Proposal
- Change Request
- Contingency
- Deviation Request
- Management Reserve
- Order of Magnitude Estimate
- Pending Change Order
- Project Variance Notice
- Performance Management Baseline
- Quantity Variation
- Revised or Current Budget

Key Points for Review

❖ **TCM Definition of Change Management**

❖ **Initiating a Change (Project Variance)**

❖ **Project Variance Notice (PVN)/Change Request**
  ○ Section 1 – Title – Use a concise title to reflect the nature of change
  ○ Section 2 – Change Information – Add a brief written description of the proposed change. Include in broad terms how the proposed change impacts the schedule in regards to appropriate work.
    ✓ The PCM/CCM or Project Controls person will assign a sequential number to the PVN, log it into the change register, and coordinate the PM review. Once the PM evaluates the PVN,

the Change Type block will be completed.
- o Section 3 – Approvals – From client and/or construction project manager
- o Section4 – Distribution – The PCM/CCM or Project Controls person will check the appropriate blocks and arrange for distribution.

❖ **PVN Review Meeting**
- o Periodic Internal Review
- o Special Internal Review
- o Client Review

❖ **Client Change Procedure**
- o Change Request Client may respond as follows:
  - ✓ Reject the proposed change request – Contractor will process the rejected change in accordance with the internal change procedure.
  - ✓ Approve the proposed change request immediately as a change order.
  - ✓ Direct that a more detailed analysis of the change be made and that it be resubmitted as a changed proposal.
- o Change Proposal –The client may respond as follows:
  - ✓ Reject the change proposal
  - ✓ Approve the change proposal as a change order

❖ **Change Order**

❖ **Contractor Internal Change Procedure**
- o Project Manager's Evaluation
- o Reject the PVN
- o Approve the PVN

❖ **Disputed Change**

❖ **Change Register**

❖ **Pending Change Order**

❖ **Change Order Identification**

Check on Learning

1. The Change Management process is not used to:

    A. Manage changes in scope
    B. Adjust baseline if the change is approved
    C. Measure productivity variations
    D. Maintain a change register

2. The Change Management Process is not used to:

    A. Approve or disapprove changes in scope
    B. Allow contractors to make up for estimate errors in the bid
    C. Close the project control cycle loop
    D. Make adjustment to the baseline

3. In the case of a disputed change, the contractor should:

    A. Ensure that subsequent actions are in accordance with contract requirements
    B. Keep separate records of the time and cost expended completing the disputed change
    C. Satisfy all notice requirements including formally disputing the change
    D. All of the above

4. Which of the following describes the Change Management Process?

    A. Flows through the contractor first, then to the client
    B. Should only be used when proposed changes are greater than $5,000
    C. Need not be used for internal changes
    D. Needs to be finalized before the project is complete

5. For an effective Change Management process:

    A. The contractor needs to follow a practical guide to manage both client and internal change
    B. The contractor needs to reserve the right to add more cost later in case a mistake is made in the initial estimate
    C. The contractor should always follow its own process so that everyone is familiar with it
    D. The contractor should issue the change request to the client as soon as it becomes aware of it

6. The contractor project manager will conduct periodic Project Variance Notice (PVN) meetings:

    A. To keep the project team fully informed
    B. They should be fairly frequent, weekly is common
    C. Each team member is to be provided prior to the meeting a variance log and a list of new variances
    D. All of the above

7. Pending change orders for which the client directs the work to proceed in advance of a written change order, approval should

    A. Not be included in a change log until they are approved
    B. If the detailed cost distribution is known costs should be tracked separately
    C. Be considered in the forecast and the budget but not in revenue
    D. Not cause the work to start until written approval is received

Solutions

1.   C   Measure productivity variations
   > Refer to Chapter 25, "Change Management Overview" topic

2.   B   Allow Contractors to make up for estimate errors in the bid
   > Refer to Chapter 25, "Change Management Overview" topic

3.   D   All of the above
   > Refer to Chapter 25, "Disputed Change" topic

4.   A   Flow through the contractor first, then to the client
   > Refer to Chapter 25, "Introduction" topic

5   A   The contractor needs to follow a practical guide to manage both client and internal change
   > Refer to Chapter 25, "General" topic

6.   D   All of the above
   > Refer to Chapter 25, "PVN Review Meetings" topic

7.   B   If the detailed cost distribution is known costs should be tracked separately
   > Refer to Chapter 25, "Pending Change Order" topic

Chapter 26 – Overview of Construction Claims and Disputes

John C. Livengood, AIA, CCP CFCC PSP FAACE
James G. Zack, Jr., CFCC FAACE AACE Hon. Life

Introduction/Learning Objectives

This chapter discusses the causes of construction claims and disputes, identifies the basic types of claims, defines the basic elements of proof of a claim in order to recover damages, and discusses what needs to be documented in order to support a claim. The chapter also outlines what are the various types of claims and how to defend against them or resolve them. The key learning objectives are:

- Understand the typical types of claims that may arise on contracts for capital projects.
- Understand what must be documented in order to successfully prepare, present, review, analyze and resolve or defend against claims.
- Understand how to successfully defend against each type of claim.
- Understand how claims arising on projects may be resolved without the need to complete the project in arbitration or litigation.

Terms to Know

- Acceleration
- Causation constructive acceleration
- Constructive change/variation
- Constructive suspension of work
- Damages/Quantum
- Delay
- Delay cost
- Differing site condition
- Direct cost
- Directed change/variation
- Field office overhead
- Force majeure
- Home office overhead
- Impact cost
- Indirect cost
- Liability/entitlement
- Lost productivity
- Suspension of Work
- Termination for convenience
- Termination for default

Key Points for Review

❖ **Changes/Variations**

- ❖ **Contractor claims**

- ❖ **Definitions**
  - o Claims
  - o Change Order/Variation Order

- ❖ **Universe of Construction Claims**
  - o Owner/Employer Directed Changes/Variations
  - o Constructive Changes/Variations
  - o Differing Site Conditions/Unforeseeable Site Conditions
  - o Directed Suspension of Work
  - o Constructive Suspension of Work
  - o Force Majeure
  - o Delay
    - ✓ Excusable, Non-Compensable Delay
    - ✓ Excusable, Compensable Delay
    - ✓ Inexcusable Delay
    - ✓ Concurrent Delay
  - o Directed Acceleration
  - o Constructive Acceleration
  - o Termination for Convenience
  - o Termination for Default

- ❖ **Owner/Employer Claims**
  - o Late Completion Damages
    - ✓ Actual Damages
    - ✓ Liquidated Damages
  - o False or Fraudulent Claims
  - o Design Deficiency or Standard of Care Claims
  - o Consequential Damages

- ❖ **Burden of Proof**
  - o Notice
  - o Liability/Entitlement
  - o Causation
  - o Damages/Quantum

- ❖ **Damages**
  - o Direct Costs
  - o Indirect Costs
    - ✓ Field office overhead
    - ✓ Home office overhead
  - o Delay Costs
  - o Impact Costs
  - o Other Contractor Damages
  - o Other Owner/Employer Damages

- ❖ **Claims and Project Delivery Methods**
  - o Unit Price
  - o Design-Bid-Build
  - o Design-Build
  - o Fast Tack Construction
  - o Multiple Prime Construction
  - o Construction Management at Risk (CM@R)
  - o Alliance Contracting/Integrated Project Delivery (IPD)
  - o Public Private Partnership (P3)

- ❖ **Analysis of a Claim**
  - o Phase One – Entitlement and Causation Analysis
  - o Phase Two – Delay Analysis
  - o Phase Three – Damage/Quantum Analysis
  - o Phase Four – Settlement Negotiations

- ❖ **Dispute Resolution**
  - o Negotiation
  - o Mediation
  - o Arbitration
  - o Litigation
  - o Alternative Dispute Resolution

Check on Learning

1. Projects that do not deal with changes/variations when they occur...

    A. Are likely to pay less for these changes/variation later
    B. Can settle changes/variations more easily in a global settlement at the end of the project
    C. Foster end of the job claims and disputes
    D. Increase the probability that these changes/variations will disappear

2. A Differing Site Condition/Unforeseeable Physical Condition clause ...

    A. Assigns all risk of latent site conditions to the contractor
    B. Is intended to alert the contractor to the risk of unanticipated site conditions so they can include an appropriate contingency cost in their bid
    C. Generally provides for direct cost damages but no delay or impact costs
    D. Assigns the risk of latent physical conditions at the site to the owner

3. A Constructive Suspension of Work ...

    A. Is an owner directive to the contractor to suspend all or a portion of the ongoing project work
    B. Is an accidental or unintended work stoppage caused by an owner/employer action or inaction which is not intended to stop work has the effect of stopping all or a portion of the work
    C. Always allows the contractor to recover lost time and delay damages
    D. Is not a legitimate basis for a claim

4. A Force Majeure is...

    A. An unforeseeable event caused by either the owner or an independent prime contractor working on the project
    B. A foreseeable event for which the contractor did not include a contingency in their bid
    C. An unforeseeable event caused by a third party or act of God over which neither the owner /employer or the contractor had any control
    D. Is a risk assigned to the contractor under the terms of the contract

5. A delay is generally defined as...

    A. An impact that causes the project to complete later than the contract's completion date
    B. An impact that causes any project activity to start or complete later than planned
    C. Any event caused by the owner that impacts any activity on the project
    D. An event which causes a loss of productivity on the site

6. Liquidated damages in a contract...

    A. Are a penalty in the event the contractor completes the project later than planned
    B. Must reflect actual damages in order to be enforceable

C. Are an estimate of the damages the owner is likely to incur if the project is completed late through no fault of the owner
D. Must be proven by the owner before they can be assessed to the contractor

7. The design-build project delivery method...

   A. Effectively precludes all claims from the contractor to the owner
   B. Assigns all risk of changes resulting from design issues to the contractor
   C. Makes no difference concerning claims from any other project delivery method
   D. Eliminates claims of design error provided that the error was not caused by inaccurate owner supplied information

8. Mediation is...

   A. A process where the mediator issues a decision which is binding on both the owner and the contractor
   B. A voluntary, consensual process whereby both the owner and the contractor submit their dispute to a neutral third party who acts as a facilitator helping the parties structure an acceptable settlement
   C. Required by most Courts as a condition precedent to initiating litigation
   D. A process where the mediator renders a temporarily binding decision which may be appealed by either the owner or the contractor to arbitration or litigation at the end of the project

9. Concurrent delay is...

   A. Two delays the started and completed on the same dates
   B. Two delays, one caused by the owner and the other by the contractor, that occur within the same update period
   C. Two nearly simultaneous delays, one of which impacts the critical path and the other consumes float on a subcritical path
   D. Two or more delays, occurring within the same timeframe, either of which would have independently impacted the critical path and which overlap each other in time to some extent

10. Constructive acceleration occurs...

    A. When a contractor is projecting late completion and decides to accelerate their work rather than pay the late completion damages under the contract
    B. When an owner / employer action or failure to act causes a contractor to complete work earlier than required or should have been required under the contract and causes a cost impact
    C. When a contractor encounters a potential delay situation and determines to work around the situation
    D. When an owner grants a time extension but does not pay delay damages

Solutions

1.   C   Owner/employers who fail to resolve changes/variations when they arise are likely to encourage large claims and disputes at the end of the job centering on unresolved issues on the project.
Refer to Chapter 26, "Changes/Variations" topic

2.   D   A Differing Site Condition/Unforeseeable Physical Condition clause is intended to transfer the risk of latent physical site conditions to the owner/employer to entice contractors to reduce contingency cost in their bids leaving the owner/employer to pay only for actual conditions encountered at the site that are materially different from those anticipated at the time of bidding.
Refer to Chapter 26, "Differing Site Conditions" topic

3.   B   A constructive suspension of work is an accidental work stoppage caused by an owner action or inaction which prevents the contractor from proceeding with all or a portion of the work.
Refer to Chapter 26, "Constructive Suspension of Work" topic

4.   C   A force majeure event is an unforeseeable event brought about by a third party or act of God over which neither the contractor not the owner/employer had any control nor was in a position to prevent.
Refer to Chapter 26, "Force Majeure" topic

5.   A   Delay is typically defined in contracts as events which impacts the project's completion date and causes the project to complete later than required by the contract.
Refer to Chapter 26, "Delays" topic

6.   C   Liquidated damages are a stipulated amount in the contract which represent owner's/ employer's estimate of the damages they are likely to incur if the project is completed late through no fault of the owner/employer, as known or estimate at the time of bidding.
Refer to Chapter 26, "Owner/Employer Claims – Liquidated Damages" topic

7.   D   The design-build project delivery method generally holds the design-build contractor liable for design errors, provided that the design error was not caused or brought about by inaccurate information provided by the owner.
Refer to Chapter 26, "Claims and Project Delivery Methods – Design-Build" topic

8.   B   Mediation is a voluntary, structured negotiation between the parties using the services of an outside, neutral facilitator who is jointly selected by both. The mediator's role is to assist the parties in reaching a mutually acceptable resolution of their issues.
Refer to Chapter 26, "Dispute Resolution - Mediation" topic

9.   D   Concurrent delay arises when there are two or more delays occurring within the same timeframe, either one of which would have on their own caused an impact to the project's critical path. To be concurrent the two delays must overlap to some extent.
Refer to Chapter 26, "Delays – Concurrent Delay" topic

10. B Constructive acceleration is caused by an owner/employer action or failure to act, which inadvertently results in a contractor being required to complete work earlier than required and results in additional costs.

Refer to Chapter 26, "Constructive Acceleration" topic

SECTION 6 – ECONOMIC ANALYSIS, STATISTICS, PROBABILITY AND RISK

Chapter 27 – Financial and Cash Flow Analysis

Scott J. Amos, PhD, PE

Introduction/Learning Objectives

The objective of this chapter is to demonstrate the framework for the modeling and subsequent analysis of cost in terms of the time value of money. The key learning objectives are:

- Calculate simple and compound interest rates, solve interest problems using basic single payments, uniform series, and gradient formulas.
- Calculate present value, future value, and equivalent uniform annual value of cash flow series.
- Calculate a cash flow for an asset investment option from a specified set of cost and revenue forecasts.
- Determine the discount rate of return of a cash flow series.
- Understand (and calculate) the concept of opportunity cost and benefits.

Terms to Know (Symbols)

- **A** - Annual amount or annuity
- **B** - Benefits or income
- **C** - Cost or expenses
- **e** - The base of natural logarithms (2.71828)
- **EOY** - End-of-year
- **EUAV** - Equivalent uniform annual value
- **F** - Future value
- **G** - Uniform or arithmetic gradient amount
- **i** – Effective annual interest rate
- **k** - Number of compound periods per year
- **MARR** - Minimum attractive rate of return
- **n** - Total number of compounding periods, or life of asset
- **P** - Present value
- **r** - Nominal annual interest rate
- **S_n** - Expected salvage value at end of year n

Key Points for Review

❖ **Interest, the time value of money**
- Simple Interest
- Compound interest
- Nominal interest rate
- Effective interest rate
- Continuous compounding

❖ **Minimum Attractive Rate of Return** - the minimum rate of return at which the owner is willing to invest

❖ **Equivalence**
  o Alternatives can only be compared at a common interest rate and common point in time

❖ **Measures of Equivalent value**
  o Present Value (PV)
  o Future Value (FV)
  o Annual Value (AV)

❖ **Discount Factors**
  o Single Payment Compound Amount Factor
  o Single Payment Present Value Factor
  o Uniform Series Sinking Fund Factor
  o Uniform Series Capital Recovery Factor
  o Uniform Series Compound Amount Factor
  o Uniform Series Present Value Factor
  o Arithmetic Gradient Present Value Factor
  o Arithmetic Gradient Uniform Series Factor

❖ **Cash Flow Conventions**
  o Cash flow diagram representations
  o Cash flow tables
  o Income/Benefits/Receipts/Salvage
  o Cost/Expenditures/Disbursements

❖ **Cash Flow Analysis Methods**
  o Equivalent Value
  o Rate-of-Return
  o Capitalized Cost
  o Benefit/Cost Ratio Analysis

❖ **Multiple Alternatives**
  o Compute the net PV, AV, or FV of each alternative at the required minimum attractive rate of return then select the alternative having the highest net PV, AV, or FV
  o Incremental Analysis using rate of return or benefit-cost ratio

Check on Learning

1. If a monthly interest rate is compounded to yield an effective 12.00 percent annual rate of return, then that monthly interest rate must be...

    A. More than 1.00 percent
    B. 1.00 percent
    C. Less than 1.00 percent
    D. None of the above is correct

2. The following chart shows end-of-period cash flows for expenses. The interest rate is 10%:

Year	Expense
1	$100
2	$100
3	$100
4	$100
5	$100

    What is the net present value of this cash flow?

    A. -$500
    B. -$269
    C. -$316.99
    D. -$379.08

3. You are evaluating an alternative that requires an initial investment of $50,000. The following chart shows end-of-period cash flows of annual savings. The interest rate is 10%.

Year	Savings
1	$ 2,667
2	$14,292
3	$19,181
4	$13,114

    What is the net present value of this investment alternative at end of year 4?

    A. -$ 746
    B. -$ 5,223
    C. -$ 9,296
    D. -$12,397

4. To finance part of an owner's new manufacturing facility, the board of directors decides to issue 2,000 bonds with a face value of $1,000, all of which are due in 15 years. The bond coupons shall pay 8% per annum, and the coupons are payable semiannually. If buyers expect a compounded 10% rate-of-return on their investment, what should they pay for the bonds?

    A. $847.89
    B. $854.30

C. $930.10
D. $943.52

(For questions 5-7) A chemical engineer obtains a 17-year patent for a new process and determines to sell it, intending to invest the proceeds for his eventual retirement. A company desires to purchase the patent and offers the engineer either of two options: (a) sell the patent rights for royalties of $20,000 per year for four years, followed by $10,000 per year for four additional years or (b) immediately sell the patent rights for a lump-sum of $85,000. The engineer estimates the weighted average annual return after taxes on his retirement investment accounts to be 11%. His effective income tax rate will be 40% for the lump-sum option and 35% for periodic payments.

5. The cash inflows for option "a" could be viewed equivalently as:

    A. $10,000 per year for years 1 through 8, plus $10,000 per year for years 1 through 4
    B. $20,000 per year for years 1 through 4, plus $10,000 per year for years 5 through 8
    C. Both A and B
    D. None of the above

6. The 11% discount rate is properly applied:

    A. After expected income taxes are deducted from the cash inflows each year
    B. Before expected income taxes are deducted from the cash inflows each year
    C. Both A and B are correct due to equivalence
    D. None of the above

7. The NPV of the after-tax cash flow for year 4 of option "a" is:

    A. $13,175
    B. $9,027
    C. $8,563
    D. None of the above is within $10 of the correct answer

(For questions 8-9) A production operation is performed with equipment on-hand and labor costs of $75,000 per year. The equipment is very low-maintenance and should last indefinitely. A new equipment item for the same operation, also very low-maintenance but requiring replacement every 6 years, can be purchased for $170,000. It will cut labor costs in half. The firm's minimum attractive rate-of-return, MARR, is 10%.

8. What option should be selected?

    A. Do nothing
    B. Replacement
    C. Either A or B may be chosen since they are equivalent
    D. Neither A or B are appropriate since the MARR is not achieved

9. For the given circumstances, what is the internal rate of return of the alternative whereby the new equipment is purchased?

   A. 9.2%
   B. 8.7%
   C. 8.2%
   D. None of the above is correct to 0.2%

10. A light electric rail line with a life estimated to be 25 years could be constructed by a city between its center and one of its suburbs at a cost of $50 million. Maintenance and operational annual costs are estimated to be $4.5 million. Benefits from improved air quality and reduced transportation costs would be $11.5 million per year, but adverse consequences to part of the population would be $2.5 million. The city must offer bonds at 8% to fund the construction. Calculate the B/C ratio if dis-benefits are taken as costs.

    A. 1.016
    B. 0.984
    C. 0.171
    D. 1.252

Solutions

1.   C   The monthly interest rate must be less than 1.00%. Were it 1.00% per month and not compounded at all, then the annual return would be 12 x 1.00% = 12.00%, which is the stated effective rate. But the monthly rate is compounded in this case, so the annual rate would exceed 12.00%, if the monthly rate were 1.00%. Since the effective annual rate is 12.00%, not more than 12.00%, the compounded monthly rate must be less than 1.00%.
Refer to Chapter 27, "Effective interest rate" topic

2.   D   The annual expense is a constant $100. This constitutes a uniform series of payments of $100 per year (A= $100). The question is to find the equivalent present value of this uniform series using (P/A, i, n) in Table 27.1. Refer to Table F.5 (at the end of Solution #10), the compound interest factor for five year (n=5) under column P/A is 3.7908. Use the following formula:

P=A (P/A, i, n) = $100* (3.7908) = $379.08. Since expense is the money out of your pocket, therefore the present value is -$379.08.
Refer to Chapter 27, "Table 27.1" topic and Table F.5

3.   D   This is an exercise of finding the present value based on a known future value each year. Since the annual savings are not equal, we will calculate the equivalent present value of each annual savings. The net cash flow will include the initial investment of $50,000 that you paid as a negative number. All savings are funds received therefore represent positive numbers. Use the formula P=F*(P/F, i, n) and compound interest factors from Appendix F.5.

P =-$50,000+$2,667*(P/F, 10%, 1) + $14,292*(P/F, 10%, 2)
    +$19,181*(P/F, 10%, 3) +$13,114*(P/F, 10%, 4)
  = -$50,000+$2,6667*(.9091) +$14,292*(.8264) +$19,181*(.7513)
   +$13,114*(.6830)
  = -$50,000+$2,424.57+$11,810.91+$14,410.69+$8,956.86
  = -$12,396.97
Refer to Chapter 27, "Equivalent net value" topic

4.   B   The bond holder will receive the full face value of the bond ($1,000) when the bond matures at the end of 15 years. In addition, the bond coupons generate a series of periodic payments to the bond holder (30 semi-annual payments). A bond buyer is only willing to pay the equivalent present value of all these future payments based on the desired rate of return (i.e. 10%).

The bond coupons will pay 8% per annum and the coupons are payable semi-annually. 8% per annum is $80 (=$1,000*.08). However, payments are made twice a year. This is equivalent to $40 every 6-months (semi-annually). We now have one lump sum future value of $1,000 face value and a uniform series of thirty (=15*2) $40 semi-annual payments. To convert these payments to present value at the desired 10 % rate of return, will involve the use of both "Single payment to present value" and "Uniform series present value."

$P = \$1,000*(P/F, 10\%, 15) + \$40*(P/A, 5\%, 30)$
$= \$1,000*(.2394) + \$40*(15.3725) = \$239.4 + \$614.9 = \$854.3$

A bond buyer expecting 10% rate of return will pay $854.3 today in exchange of a bond for $1,000 received at the end of 15 years and thirty $40 payments received semi-annually.

Note: Since coupons are payable semi-annually, the compound interest factor will be treated as n=15*2=30 but discounted at half of the desired rate of return (5%=10%/2).
Refer to Chapter 27, "Equivalent net value" topic & Example 27.5

5.   C   The cash flows in any year can be grouped or "broken down" in any manner that will ease the cost engineer's task in applying standard engineering economy calculation factors. If applying present value formulas, it is generally easier to structure cash flows to run without interruption from the present and for whatever number of years is in the period of study or comparison, than it is to have broken, staggered, or incomplete series of cash flows. Note that viewing the cash flows of the problem as $10,000 for 8 years, plus $10,000 for years 1 through 4 offers a somewhat simpler formulation than does viewing the flows as $20,000 for years 1 through 4, plus $10,000 for years 5 through 8. In the latter case, the cost engineer must apply a present value factor (discounting Year 4 to present) to the uniform payment series present value factor (discounting annual payments to a Year 4 value) for cash flows of Years 5 through 8.

Validation:
$\$10,000 \, (P/A, i, 8) + \$10,000 \, (P/A, i, 4) = \$10,000 \, (P/A, 10\%, 8) + \$10,000 \, (P/A, 10\%, 4)$
$= \$10,000*(.53349) + \$10,000*(.3.1699) = \$53,349 + \$31,699 = \$85,048$

$\$20,000 \, (P/A, i, 4) + \$10,000 \, (P/A, i, 4) \times (P/F, i, 4)$
$= \$20,000 \, (P/A, 10\%, 4) + \$10,000 \, (P/A, 10\%, 4) \times (P/F, 10\%, 4)$
$= \$20,000 \, (3.1699) + \$10,000 \, (3.1699) \times (.683) = \$63,398 + \$21,650 = \$85,048$
Refer to Chapter 27, "Equivalent net value" topic

6.   A   The 11% rate is stated to be the return "after taxes." By definition, an after-tax rate of return refers to a discount rate determined or applied after any required taxes have been subtracted from all cash flows of the alternative. If that rate, the only one stated in the problem, is to be applied as the discount rate for net present value comparisons, then the cash flows of any alternatives so compared must be adjusted to be "after taxes."
Refer to Chapter 27, "Multiple alternatives" topic

7.   C   Year 4 of option "a" yields a payment of $20,000, minus the 35% tax payment.

Net cash flow $_4$ = $20,000 – (35% x $20,000) = $13,000

That net flow must be discounted at the 11% after-tax rate of return, using the present value factor, P/F.

$NPV_4 = \$13,000 \, (P/F, 11\%, 4) = \$13,000*(.6587) = \$8,563$

Refer to Chapter 27, "Equivalent net value" topic

8.   A   There are two alternatives that must be compared: "do-nothing" to replace the existing equipment item, or purchase the replacement item. Presumably, since nothing was stated about differing efficiencies of production, the production offered by each item is the same, and costs are all that need be compared. The period of comparison should be the 6-year replacement period.

PV of costs without replacement:
-$75,000 $(P/A, 10\%, 6)$ = -$75,000*(4.3553) = -$326,648

PV of costs with replacement (purchase price, but half of the annual labor costs):
-$170,000 - $37,500 $(P/A, 10\%, 6)$ = -$170,000 - $163,324 = -$333,324

Since costs are greater if the replacement is purchased, replacement is inappropriate. One can obtain the same result by looking at the problem differently. Buying the replacement at a cost of $170,000 offers savings of $37,500 in labor costs for each of the 6 years in the period of study. Is the NPV of this alternative a positive value?

NPV = -$170,000 + $37,500 $(P/A, 10\%, 6)$ = -$170,000 + $163,324
        = -$6,676

Since NPV < 0, replacement is inappropriate. In yet a third way, the cost engineer can compare annualized cash flows to obtain the same decision. By this technique the $37,500 annual labor savings is compared to the equivalent annualized cost of the equipment replacement:

NAV = -$170,000 $(A/P, 10\%, 6)$ = -$170,000*(.2296) = -$39,032

Since the $37,500 annual labor savings is less than the $39,032 annualized cost of the replacement equipment purchase, it would be inappropriate to purchase the item.
                    Refer to Chapter 27, "Multiple alternatives" topic

9.   B   The internal rate of return, IRR, is the discount rate that results in NPV = 0 for the cash flows. Determining the IRR is easy with a financial calculator. Entries for a financial calculator (HP-12C, for example) would be:

PV = -$170,000; PMT = $37,500; n = 6; solve for i to obtain i = IRR = 8.648%
(Warning: if using a financial calculator on the certification examination, one should be sure to know its operations thoroughly *before* the test.)

Those without such a calculator must resort to an iterative, trial-and-error approach, substituting assorted discount rates until NPV = 0 = -$170,000 + $37,500 $(P/A, i, 6)$. It often makes sense to begin with the MARR (if known) for the unknown i, obtain the NPV, and then see whether the unknown i is greater or less than the substituted value.

NPV = -$170,000 + $37,500 $(P/A, 10\%, 6)$ = -$6,676

To raise the NPV to zero, the future $37,500 cash flows should not be discounted so heavily. That is, a lower discount rate is necessary to give the future cash inflows more value and increase the NPV to zero. To determine approximately how much to decrease the IRR, look at the NPV = -$6,676. Divided by 6 years, the -$6,676 is -$1,113 per year. Compare the -$1,113 per year to the annual $37,500: $1,113 ÷ $37,500 = 2.97%, about 3%. It would seem that decreasing the 10% to 7% should bring the NPV closer to zero, or at least allow the correct discount rate to be bracketed, so that it can be accurately approximated by interpolation.

NPV = -$170,000 + $37,500 (P/A, 7%, 6) = -$170,000 + $37,500*(4.7665)
    = -$170,000 + 178,744 = $8,744

With NPV's on both sides of zero, linear interpolation is now possible. (Recognize that the relationships are not perfectly linear, only approximately so.) The NPV ranges from $8,744 to -$6,676, a total of $15,420. That dollar range corresponds to the discount rate range from 7% to 10%, a total of 3%. The $15,420 ÷ 3% yields $5,140 NPV change for each 1% of discount rate change. The discount rate percentage change that increases the 7% rate to the IRR should be about:

$8,744 ÷ $5,140 = 1.7%

The interpolation reveals that the IRR should approximate 7% + 1.7% = 8.7%. From the accurate financial calculator result of IRR = 8.648%, the 8.7% approximation for the IRR is reasonably accurate.

Refer to Chapter 27, "Rate of Return" topic & Example 27.10

10. B   The B/C ratio can be expressed in terms of present values or annual values. Since all values except initial cost are expressed on an annual basis, the simple solution is to convert the $50 million to an annual amount using:

A= P (A/P, i, n) = $50,000,000 (A/P, 8%, 25) = $50,000,000(.0937) = $4.685 million
Then
Benefits = $11.5 million

Adding all of the costs and dis-benefits,
Costs = $4.685 + $4.5 + $2.5 = $11.685 million

The B/C ratio = $11.5/$11.685 = 0.984 which is not an acceptable ratio.

Refer to Chapter 27, "Benefit-Cost Ratio Incremental Analysis" topic

Table F.5 Compound Interest Discount Factors at Ten Percent

n	F/P	P/F	A/F	A/P	F/A	P/A	A/G	P/G
1	1.1000	0.9091	1.0000	1.1000	1.0000	0.9091	0.0000	0.0000
2	1.2100	0.8264	0.4762	0.5762	2.1000	1.7355	0.4762	0.8264
3	1.3310	0.7513	0.3021	0.4021	3.3100	2.4869	0.9366	2.3291
4	1.4641	0.6830	0.2155	0.3155	4.6410	3.1699	1.3812	4.3781
5	1.6105	0.6209	0.1638	0.2638	6.1051	3.7908	1.8101	6.8618
6	1.7716	0.5645	0.1296	0.2296	7.7156	4.3553	2.2236	9.6842
7	1.9487	0.5132	0.1054	0.2054	9.4872	4.8684	2.6216	12.7631
8	2.1436	0.4665	0.0874	0.1874	11.4359	5.3349	3.0045	16.0287
9	2.3579	0.4241	0.0736	0.1736	13.5795	5.7590	3.3724	19.4215
10	2.5937	0.3855	0.0627	0.1627	15.9374	6.1446	3.7255	22.8913
11	2.8531	0.3505	0.0540	0.1540	18.5312	6.4951	4.0641	26.3963
12	3.1384	0.3186	0.0468	0.1468	21.3843	6.8137	4.3884	29.9012
13	3.4523	0.2897	0.0408	0.1408	24.5227	7.1034	4.6988	33.3772
14	3.7975	0.2633	0.0357	0.1357	27.9750	7.3667	4.9955	36.8005
15	4.1772	0.2394	0.0315	0.1315	31.7725	7.6061	5.2789	40.1520

Table F.4 Compound Interest Discount Factors at Eight Percent

n	F/P	P/F	A/F	A/P	F/A	P/A	A/G	P/G
1	1.0800	0.9259	1.0000	1.0800	1.0000	0.9259	0.0000	0.0000
2	1.1664	0.8573	0.4808	0.5608	2.0800	1.7833	0.4808	0.8573
3	1.2597	0.7938	0.3080	0.3880	3.2464	2.5771	0.9487	2.4450
4	1.3605	0.7350	0.2219	0.3019	4.5061	3.3121	1.4040	4.6501
5	1.4693	0.6806	0.1705	0.2505	5.8666	3.9927	1.8465	7.3724
6	1.5869	0.6302	0.1363	0.2163	7.3359	4.6229	2.2763	10.5233
7	1.7138	0.5835	0.1121	0.1921	8.9228	5.2064	2.6937	14.0242
8	1.8509	0.5403	0.0940	0.1740	10.6366	5.7466	3.0985	17.8061
9	1.9990	0.5002	0.0801	0.1601	12.4876	6.2469	3.4910	21.8081
10	2.1589	0.4632	0.0690	0.1490	14.4866	6.7101	3.8713	25.9768
11	2.3316	0.4289	0.0601	0.1401	16.6455	7.1390	4.2395	30.2657
12	2.5182	0.3971	0.0527	0.1327	18.9771	7.5361	4.5957	34.6339
13	2.7196	0.3677	0.0465	0.1265	21.4953	7.9038	4.9402	39.0463
14	2.9372	0.3405	0.0413	0.1213	24.2149	8.2442	5.2731	43.4723
15	3.1722	0.3152	0.0368	0.1168	27.1521	8.5595	5.5945	47.8857
16	3.4259	0.2919	0.0330	0.1130	30.3243	8.8514	5.9046	52.2640
17	3.7000	0.2703	0.0296	0.1096	33.7502	9.1216	6.2037	56.5883
18	3.9960	0.2502	0.0267	0.1067	37.4502	9.3719	6.4920	60.8426
19	4.3157	0.2317	0.0241	0.1041	41.4463	9.6036	6.7697	65.0134
20	4.6610	0.2145	0.0219	0.1019	45.7620	9.8181	7.0369	69.0898
21	5.0338	0.1987	0.0198	0.0998	50.4229	10.0168	7.2940	73.0629
22	5.4365	0.1839	0.0180	0.0980	55.4568	10.2007	7.5412	76.9257
23	5.8715	0.1703	0.0164	0.0964	60.8933	10.3711	7.7786	80.6726
24	6.3412	0.1577	0.0150	0.0950	66.7648	10.5288	8.0066	84.2997
25	6.8485	0.1460	0.0137	0.0937	73.1059	10.6748	8.2254	87.8041

Chapter 28 – Practical Corporate Investment Decision-Making Guide

James D. Whiteside, II, PE FAACE

Introduction/Learning Objectives

The objective of this chapter is to identify the key concepts and details necessary to translate project economics into fundamental parameters to assist executives in investment decision making. This chapter provides the structure required for a Project Assessment Document (PAD) with explanation and examples of the technical requirements for each section. The key learning objectives are:

- Understand the importance of a transparent and objective summary to investment decision makers.
- Understand the importance of the lost profit opportunity (LPO) on the economics of a proposed project.
- Understand why the Average Annual Rate of Return (AARR) is preferred over a simple Return on Investment (ROI) and the relationship of AARR is to LPO.
- Identify the basic steps to investment decision making.
- Understand how a company utilizes the portfolio management process to decide which project(s) to fund.
- Identify the seven key elements to an executive summary.
- Understand how the variances to non-controllable and controllable expenses affect the project cost forecast.
- Identify factors and their individual effects on the AARR.
- Understand the need for using a cash flow curve to include risks associated with economic, financial, and political risks to develop a forecast of the projects' revenue generation life cycle.
- Present revenue breakdown of the sale price per unit in order to place profit in context of the operating and material costs.
- Present economic indicators in a standard industry format to assess the project with respect to industry benchmarks.
- Understand risks to annual revenue generation and why it is important to understand the risks to cash flow.
- Understand how projects are selected to manage a corporation's cash flow and strategic vision.

Terms to Know (Symbols)

- **AARR** – Average Annual Rate of Return
- **CAPEX** – Capital Expenditure
- **FEED** – Front-End Engineering and Design
- **FEL** – Front-End Loading
- **FX** – Foreign Exchange
- **LPO** – Lost Profit Opportunity
- **NPV** – Net Present Value
- **OPEX** – Operating Expenditure

- **PAD** – Project Assessment Document
- **PI** – Profitability Index
- **ROCE** – Return on Capital Employed
- **ROI** – Return On Investment
- **ROR** – Return On Revenue

Key Points for Review

- ❖ **Cash Flow Analysis**
  - o Economic Risks
  - o Financial Risks
  - o Political Risks

- ❖ **Drivers**
  - o Technical Issues
  - o Commercial Issues

- ❖ **Economic Summary**
  - o Economic Premises
  - o Base Case Economic Indicators

- ❖ **Important Elements Required by Investment Decision-Makers**
  - o Value to the company
  - o Effect on cash flow
  - o Transparency of the risk to the company

- ❖ **Investment Decision-Making Steps**
  - o Setting strategy and analysis
  - o Establishing a risk/return on goals
  - o Searching for investment opportunities
  - o Forecasting expected costs and returns
  - o Evaluating forecast returns
  - o Assessing and adjusting for risk
  - o Making the decision to act
  - o Implementing accepted proposals
  - o Auditing operating performance
  - o Managing the asset and
  - o Terminating the asset

- ❖ **Lost Profit Opportunity (Terms of similar concept):**
  - o Opportunity Loss or Cost
  - o Economic Profit (or Loss)
  - o Recovery Lost Profits
  - o Lost Profits and Damages
  - o Asset Utilization

- ❖ **Project Drivers**
  - o Capital

- Revenue
- Operating
- Schedule

❖ **Portfolio Management Process**
  - Inputs: Investor Objectives, Market Conditions
  - Output: Portfolio Performance Measurement
  - Monitoring and Rebalancing: Targets, Strategy, Objectives, Expectations

❖ **Seven Key Elements to an Executive Summary**
  - Statement of the problem that the project addresses
  - Project Summary
  - Key Project Drivers
  - Primary Risks and Uncertainties
  - Capital Cost Variance
  - Average Annual Rate of Return
  - Cash Flow Analysis

Check on Learning

1. What is a discount rate used in economic assessment for a project?

    A. It must be greater than 13%
    B. It is the value of the financing percentage to get a loan
    C. The rate that must be earned to satisfy the rate of return required by company investors
    D. None of the above is correct

2. Which discount rate should be used for decision making of a project?

    A. The company (business unit or subsidiary) discount rate
    B. The corporation's discount rate
    C. The bare cost of capital
    D. The value of the loan required to pay the project out in 7 to 10 years

3. A company will have a cash flow shortfall of $10 million per year starting in four years. A company has 2 projects to choose for funding. The investors have expressed discontent at annual stockholder meetings that the company's projects do not make more return on investment. Which project should the company choose for funding?

    A. Project 1:

        AARR of 15%
        Funding request is $400 million
        Will generate $45 million profit per year starting in Year 8 of operation

    B. Project 2:

        AARR is 5%
        Funding request is $400 million
        Will generate $15 million profit per year starting in Year 5 of operation

    C. Both Projects 1 and 2 can be ready for startup in 3 years from today

4. The primary reason for a corporation to select a project is based on:

    A. The cash flow of the project
    B. Projects are necessary to justify project staffing requirements
    C. To meet the investor's objectives
    D. The cash flow of the corporation and alignment with the corporation's objectives

5. Which project site would be the first choice for a corporation?

    A. Site A:
        Adjoining an existing site
        High tax rate
        Moderate productivity

Low wages
Stable Government

B. Site B
New country
Low tax rate
Moderate productivity
Moderate wages
New market
Government faces economic problems

C. Site C- Adjoining an existing site
High tax rate
Moderate productivity
Moderate wages
New Government

D. Site D
Site is located in an existing industrial park
Tax break for first 15 years of operation
Moderate productivity
High wages
Stable Government (military involved)

6. Investment Decision Schedule drivers include dates for:

   A. FEL, engineering, procurement and construction
   B. Partner negotiations, sanctioning approval, permits granted, and full production
   C. Critical path items such as compressors that have long delivery times
   D. Technical issues about how risk scenarios were addressed

7. An outside investor is reviewing companies for long term stability with solid returns. Which company would be best to choose for investing?

   A. Company A
      ROCE: 25%
      Average Project IRR: 15%

   B. Company B
      ROCE: 15%
      Average Project IRR: 18%

   C. Company C
      ROCE: 10%
      Average Project IRR: 35%

   D. A or B

8. The discount rate for the corporation is 12%. The yearly profits for the first six years of operation after deducting tax, labor, materials, and transportation costs are shown below. Which project should be considered first?

A. Project A
Final Cost = USD$210,500,000

Year	Yearly Profit (USD$)
1	12,000,000
2	14,000,000
3	12,000,000
4	19,000,000
5	22,000,000
6	18,000,000
Total Profit	USD $97,000,000

B. Project B
Final Cost = USD$175,000,000

Year	Yearly Profit (USD$
1	12,000,000
2	14,000,000
3	12,000,000
4	18,000,000
5	22,000,000
6	12,000,000
Total Profit	USD $90,000,000

C. Project C
Final Cost = USD$145,000,000

Year	Yearly Profit (USD$)
1	12,000,000
2	14,000,000
3	12,000,000
4	18,000,000
5	22,000,000
6	12,000,000
Total Profit	USD $90,000,000

D. Project D
Final Cost = USD$123,000,000

Year	Yearly Profit (USD$)
1	12,000,000
2	14,000,000
3	12,000,000
4	17,000,000
5	21,000,000
6	6,000,000
Total Profit	USD $82,000,000

9. In order to effectively communicate the transparency of true cost of a project for funding, the team should:

   A. Create a capital cost variance graphic that illustrates the effect of controllable and uncontrollable costs to a possible worst-case scenario
   B. Include both controllable and uncontrollable costs in a forecast cost
   C. Include only controllable costs in the forecast
   D. Only provide an estimate based on the NPV of the project, along with the contingency and escalation amounts

10. If the AARR for a project drops from 15% at funding to 10% at the time the project is ready for startup, then the potential profit loss over a life span of 20 years is:

   A. Negligible
   B. Can be offset by running the facility over its design limit for a few years to make up for project cost overrun
   C. May exceed 75% of the final cost of the project
   D. Can be moved to an expense ledger for a tax write-off

Solutions

1.   C   While 13% is generally accepted as "the discount rate" for industry, it varies depending on the industry sector. The discount rate must satisfy the rate of return required by company investors. They are investing money to make an expected return on their investment and their investment may be a significant funding component for the project.
Refer to Chapter 28, "Average Annual Rate of Return" topic

2.   B   A corporation that has more stable cash flows has a better risk profile than a company (business unit or subsidiary) that has cash flows that might vary a lot. The more diversified a corporation is, the more stable is its cash flows; if one project underperforms, there might be another project that compensates.
Refer to Chapter 28, "Average Annual Rate of Return" topic

3.   B   Neither project is going to completely solve the cash flow problem that the company faces in four years. However, Project 2 starts generating profit sooner than Project 1 by 3 years. The company will need to continue to look for other opportunities to resolve its cash flow problem.
Refer to Chapter 28, "Cash Flow Analysis" topic

4.   D   The cash flow of the project is not as important as the cash flow that the project contributes to the cash flow of the corporation. Corporations have to analyze which project will contribute to sustain the cash flow of the corporation. While the investor's objectives are important consideration, their objectives might be short-term interests. Corporations must make strategic decisions to meet long-term objectives of where they want to be in the market place.
Refer to Chapter 28, "Portfolio Management Process" topic

5.   A   The choice for project consideration is the site that has the lowest risk to the cash flow of the corporation based on economic, financial, and political risks. The suggested solution is to use a risk matrix. Assign each of the criteria: "H" for high risk, "M" for a moderate risk, and "L" for a low risk. Prioritize the projects by the number of risks in each category. Site A has the most low risks associated with the site and should be the first choice to consider.

Risk Matrix				
Site	High	Moderate	Low	Priority
A	1	1	3	1
B	3	2	1	4
C	2	2	1	3
D	1	3	1	2

Refer to Chapter 28, "Risk to Revenue Generation" topic

6.   B   Investment decisions are made on schedule dates associated with development planning and project execution dates. The other answers are drivers that are of interest to project professionals. However, the investment decision makers trust that the project management professionals have performed the necessary work to address the other tasks before bringing the project in for review.
Refer to Chapter 28, "Schedule Drivers" topic

7.   D   The answer ("D") is that Company A or Company B are good choices for "long term, stable" investments. Company A has mature assets that are now depreciating and the company is generating revenue (the ROCE is higher than the IRR). Company B is "living within their means" because their IRR is slightly higher than their ROCE. Company C has no assets and is simply generating high returns on projects. This is a risky position because they have no assets to sell or leverage if a project or series of projects overrun.
Refer to Chapter 28, "Base Case Economic Indicators" topic

8.   D   The answer is to calculate the Average Annual Rate of Return (AARR). The project should have an AARR that is higher than the discount rate of the company. While project C has an AARR of 10.38 and project D is 11.11, they are essentially the same answer. None of the answers meet the 12% discount rate requirement for the corporation. Answers are not a result of point calculations. There is an accuracy range around any given calculation and there must be some analysis of the data used in the calculations. Answer C has a profit spike in Year 5. It is risky to accept a solution that is dependent on one year having stellar performance. Answer D has the least risk because the profit from year to year is gradually increasing. Further, the profit in Year 6 is very low and may be an indication of planned maintenance costs. Answer D may be based on operational planning and Answer C is more of a business development answer.

Project D AARR = 11.11
Refer to Chapter 28, "Average Annual Rate of Return" topic

9.   A   Create a capital cost variance graphic that illustrates the effect of controllable and uncontrollable costs to a possible worst-case scenario. Along with this graph should be a description of the magnitude of risk associated with each cost variance. Given that two projects may have the same NPV and cost variances, the project with less risk may be a better choice for the investment decision.
Refer to Chapter 28, "Capital Drivers" topic

10.   C   The final cost of the project is part of the AARR calculation. Generally, projects overrun their original budgets and when they do, the effect on the AARR is significant. Cost overruns are generally a result of design and construction changes that may also affect the first few years of operations when it is critical for the project to achieve the design rating. Loss of production means loss of market and a longer payout. The result typically means the capital costs associated to fix operating issues, design issues, etc. can be very significant. The additional costs to get the project to maintain design specification are part of the corporation's assessment of AARR for the project.
Refer to Chapter 28, "Average Annual Rate of Return" topic

Chapter 29 – Statistics & Probability

Elizabeth Y. Chen PhD
Mark T. Chen PE CCP FAACE AACE Hon. Life

Introduction/Learning Objectives

Statistics is the field of study where data are collected for the purpose of drawing conclusions and making inferences. Probability is used to analyze the potential outcome of an endeavor such as contract bidding. The key learning objectives are:

- Understand basic definitions and terminologies in probability and statistics.
- Apply statistical techniques in decision making.
- Understand the basic concept of regression analysis.

Terms to Know

- Expected Value
- Frequency Distribution
- Mean (average)
- Median
- Mode
- Normal Distribution
- Population
- Probability Distribution
- Random Variable
- Range
- Regression Analysis
- Sample
- Standard Deviation
- Variance

Key Points for Review

❖ **Description of quantitative data**
  o Graphic methods:
    ✓ frequency distribution; relative frequency(f/n)
    ✓ stem and leaf plots
    ✓ histogram

  o Numerical methods: Measures of location (central tendency)
    ✓ Mean (average)
    ✓ Median
    ✓ Mode

Measures of dispersion
- ✓ Range
- ✓ Variance
- ✓ Standard deviation

❖ **Relative standing**
- o pth percentile
- o Z-score

❖ **Binomial Distribution**

❖ **Normal Distribution**

❖ **Standard Normal Distribution**

❖ **Regression Analysis**
- o Linear Regression
- o Multiple Regression

Check on Learning

1. A charity organization is seeking help to analyze the contribution pattern. The objective is to develop the budget to fund worthy projects. You as a volunteer from AACE International are being called upon to share your expertise. The first step is analyzing contribution checks received. You have randomly selected ten checks with the following contribution amounts:

    $15, $10, $25, $10, $5, $10, $30, $20, $10, $15

    a. What is the Mean (Average) of these contributions?

    A. $17.5
    B. $15
    C. $12.5
    D. $10

    b. What is the "Median" contribution amount?

    A. $10
    B. $15
    C. $12.5
    D. $17.5

    c. What is the "Mode" of contribution amount?

    A. $5
    B. $10
    C. $15
    D. $30

    d. What is the range of contributions?

    A. $25
    B. $15
    C. $5
    D. $20

    e. What is the variance of the contributions?

    A. 68.06
    B. 55
    C. 61.11
    D. 88.89

    f. What is the standard deviation?

    A. $8.25
    B. $7.82

C. $7.42
D. $9.43

2. The organization is interested in measuring the dispersion of these contributions. Which one of the following suggestions will not reveal this information?

   A. Average the deviations of each contribution from the mean
   B. Variance
   C. Standard deviation
   D. Range

3. A random variable that can assume any value within some interval or intervals is called --

   A. Continuous random variable
   B. Discrete random variable
   C. Binomial random variable
   D. Normal random variable

4. A contractor specializes in completing small homes in 60 days. For each home completed on schedule he earns $5,000. A $10,000 penalty is assessed on the contractor if the home is completed longer than 60 days. From his past experience, the odds are 8 out 10 times with on time completion. If the contractor were to build a large number of homes, what is his expected value of gain or loss per home?

   A. -$2,000
   B. -$5,000
   C. $2,000
   D. $5,000

5. Which one of the following statements is incorrect regarding the normal distribution?

   A. It is bell-shaped and is symmetrical about the mean
   B. All probability distributions resemble normal curves
   C. The probability density function curve approaches but never touches the horizontal axis
   D. Almost all observations are within +3 and -3 standard deviations

6. Which one of the following statements is incorrect regarding the regression analysis?

   A. A tool to estimate the parameters of the adopted probability model
   B. Only one model could be developed from a given set of observed (historical) data
   C. The analysis provides an approximation to illustrate how closely the model is able to predict or estimate the dependent variable
   D. The model that yields the minimum SSE (sum of squared error) is chosen as the best fit

Solution

1a.   B   Mean = Sum of all numbers in the sample / n (Number of sample data)
= ($15+$10+$25+$10+$5+$10+$30+$20+$10+$15)/10 = $150/10 = $15
        Refer to Chapter 29, "Mean" topic

1b.   C   The contribution amounts are re-arranged from the smallest to the largest amount as follows:
$5, $10, $10, $10, $10, $15, $15, $20, $25, $30

Since there is even number of data, the median is the average of the two middle data points (5th & 6th data).
Median = ($10+$15)/2 = $12.5
        Refer to Chapter 29, "Median" topic

1c.   B   Mode is the contribution that occurs most often in the sample data
Mode = $10 since $10 appears most often (four times)
        Refer to Chapter 29, "Mode" topic

1d.   A   Range is the difference between the largest ($30) and the smallest ($5) contributions.
Range = $30-$5 = $25
        Refer to Chapter 29, "Range" topic

1e.   C   Variance = (Sum of (Each contribution – Mean) ^ 2)/(n-1)
= ((5-15)^2+(10-15)^2+(10-15)^2+(10-15)^2+(10-15)^2+(15-15)^2+(15-15)^2+
(20-15)^2+(25-15)^2+(30-15)^2)/(10-1)
= (100+25+25+25+25+0+0+25+100+225)/(10-1)
= 550/9 = 61.11
        Refer to Chapter 29, "Variance" topic

1f.   B   Standard Deviation = Sq root of Variance = Sq root of 61.11 = 7.82
        Refer to Chapter 29, "Standard Deviation" topic

2.   A   Continuous random variable can assume any value within intervals.
        Refer to Chapter 29, "Continuous Random Variables" topic

3.   C   The expected value = $5000(8/10) + (-$10000(2/10)) = $4000 – $2000 = $2000
        Refer to Chapter 29, "Probability Distribution & Example C" topic

4.   B   Majority of the probability distributions resembles a normal curve but not all. For
                example, a triangular distribution is sometimes used in risk analysis
                        Refer to Chapter 29, "The Normal Distribution" topic

5.   B   Several models could be developed from a given set of observed (historical) data
                        Refer to Chapter 29, "Regression Analysis" topic

Chapter 30 – Optimization

Dr. Robert C. Creese, PE CCP

Introduction/Learning Objectives

Optimization is a process of determining the best or most effective result utilizing a quantitative measurement system using variables such as currency, time, or quantity of materials. Typical applications of the optimization include maximizing profit, minimizing construction time, maximizing production, minimizing labor cost etc. The key learning objectives are:

- Understanding how to develop a valid model of the system to be optimized.
- Gaining familiarity with linear programming and solving a simple linear programming problem.
- Being able to perform simple Monte Carlo simulation.
- Applying sensitivity analysis to support decision-making.

Terms to Know

- Linear Programming
- Modeling
- Monte Carlo Simulation
- Sensitivity Analysis

Key Points for Review

❖ **Modeling**
  o Mathematical relationship of the desired performance and the independent variables
  o Used when it is impractical or cost prohibitive to directly measure performance

❖ **Linear Programming**
  o Linear objective function
  o Linear constraints
  o Activities

❖ **Monte Carlo Simulation**
  o Sampling technique to simulate real life or to make predictions
  o Random numbers
  o Simulation result vs. expected value

❖ **Sensitivity Analysis**
  o Test how the performance is impacted by changes of variables
  o Identify which variable has the greatest performance impact

Check on Learning

1. Which type of models is not considered to be engineering models?

    A. Linear Programming
    B. Queuing
    C. Fashion
    D. Monte Carlo Simulation

2. Models are simplified representations of reality by_____ systems which are used to optimize the performance of real systems.

    A. Redundant
    B. Simple or Complex
    C. Electrical
    D. Maintenance

3. Which type of models develops complex relationships that are difficult to explain between the input and output, but predict results that are accurate?

    A. Linear Programming
    B. Queuing
    C. Linear Regression
    D. Neural Network

4. Monte Carlo Simulation is based upon the generation of _____ numbers.

    A. Real
    B. Imaginary
    C. Random
    D. Complex

5. A contractor wants to maximize the profits in building a new development. The contractor has 15 acres available and the expensive houses require 1.4 acres and the economical houses require 1.0 acres. The profits are $ 80,000 for the expensive house and $ 50,000 for the economical house. The costs to build the houses are $ 0.90 million for the expensive house and $ 0.50 million for the economical house and the contractor can obtain only $ 9 million from the bank. How many completed houses (no fractional houses) of each type should the contractor build to maximize her/his profits? It is suggested that the student use the Excel® add-in "Solver" for the solution of the problem.

    a. How many of each house should the contractor build?

        A. Expensive 10   Economical 0
        B. Expensive 7   Economical 4
        C. Expensive 6   Economical 6
        D. Expensive 7   Economical 5

b. How much profit will the contractor likely make?

    A. $750,000
    B. $800,000
    C. $810,000
    D. $780,000

6. A construction company has obtained a contract for 8 million dollars. The contractor estimates that the total project cost will follow the following distribution:

Project Cost (million dollars)	Probability of that cost
5.5	0.05
6.0	0.05
6.5	0.25
7.0	0.10
7.5	0.30
8.0	0.05
8.5	0.05
9.0	0.15

a. Calculate the mean value of the costs._____

    A. 6.955
    B. 6.875
    C. 7.500
    D. 7.325

b. Determine the range of the profits from the contract in million dollar units.

    A. 5.5 to 9.0
    B. -1.0 to 2.5
    C. 6.5 to 7.5
    D. 0.5 to 1.5

Solutions

1.   C   Fashion
                Refer to Chapter 30, "Introduction" topic

2.   B   Simple or Complex
                Refer to Chapter 30, "Modeling" topic

3.   D   Neural Network
                Refer to Chapter 30, "Modeling" topic

4.   C   Random
                Refer to Chapter 30, "Monte Carlo Simulation" topic

5a.   D   Expensive 7, Economical 5
                Refer to Chapter 30, "Example Problem: Developer Decision" topic

5b.   C $810,000
                Refer to Chapter 30, "Example Problem: Developer Decision" topic

6a.   D   7.325
                Refer to Chapter 30, "Monte Carlo Simulation" topic

6b.   B   -1.0 to 2.5-
                Refer to Chapter 30, "Monte Carlo Simulation" topic

Problem 9: Detailed Solution

5a. Set-up Problem

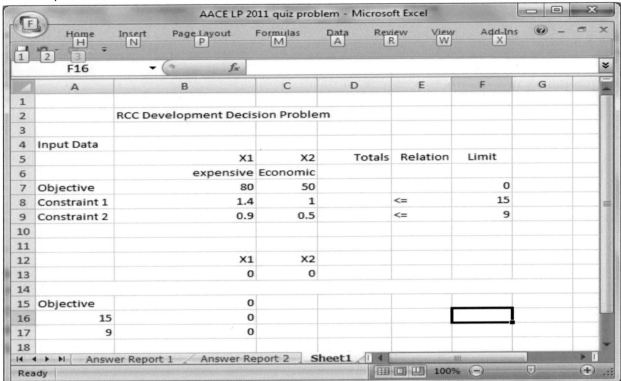

5a. Problem Solution

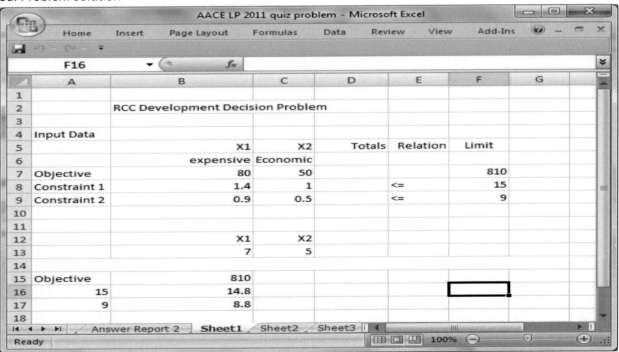

Problem 10: Detailed Solution

6a.   D   Mean Value = 5.5*0.05+ 6.0*0.05+ 6.5*0.25+ 7.0*0.10+ 7.5*0.30+ 8.0*0.05+ 8.5*0.05+ 9.0*0.15 = 7.325

6b.   B   Range of costs= Minimum to Maximum values, 5.5-9.0 Million. Since contract is for 8 million, then the range of the profits is 8 – cost range = (8-9) to (8-5.5) = -1.0 to +2.5 million

Chapter 31 – Risk Management Fundamentals

Allen C. Hamilton, CCP

Introduction/Learning Objectives

Risk management is an important tool in the management of projects. The fundamental approach to risk management is to identify the risks to project success, assess and analyze the risks, and develop plans to control the risks. Risk management follows the sequence: Plan, Assess, Treat, and Control. This chapter provides an overview of the process and examples of how to apply the tools of risk management. The key learning objectives are:

- Understand risk management.
- Identify techniques for identifying risk, assessing risk occurrence and impact, and analyzing risk.
- Understand risk treatment.
- Perform quantitative risk analyses (i.e. simulation, sensitivity analysis, and decision trees).
- Understand risk analysis software.
- Describe the use of contingency.

Terms to Know

- Contingency
- Decision Tree
- Decision Tree Analysis
- Quantitative Risk Analysis
- Risk
- Risk Analysis
- Risk Assessment
- Risk Control
- Risk Identification
- Risk Management
- Risk Planning
- Risk Treatment
- Sensitivity Analysis
- Simulation

Key Points for Review

❖ **Risk Management Steps**
  o Risk Planning
    ✓ Establish the approach, form, content
    ✓ Define results of risk management
    ✓ Define key terms
    ✓ Establish criteria for risk identification and assessment, analysis approaches and general risk treatment strategies
  o Risk Assessment

- ✓ Elements of risk identification
- ✓ Assemble a list of project risks
- ✓ Internal and External Risks
  - ▪ Internal Risk: Management problem, schedule delays, cost overruns, technical/quality problems, etc.
  - ▪ External Risks: Natural hazards, new or revised government regulations, market conditions, legal, technical, etc.
- o Risk Treatment
  - ✓ Relative importance and impact of the risk item
  - ✓ Probability of occurrence: High, medium, and low
  - ✓ Potential Impact: High, medium, and low
  - ✓ Analysis
    - ▪ Review on the consistence of risk items
    - ▪ Selection of risk items for treatment (the occurrence/impact matrix)
- o Risk Control
  - ✓ Methods of handling risk: Avoidance, prevention, reduction, transfer, hedging, insurance
  - ✓ Judgment of cost to treat and the probability of success
  - ✓ Accountability of treatment
  - ✓ Follow-up

- ❖ **Quantitative Risk Analysis**
  - o Simulation (Monte Carlo) steps
    - ✓ Develop a model
    - ✓ Select the group for analysis
    - ✓ Identify uncertainty
    - ✓ Analyze the model with simulation
    - ✓ Generate reports and analyze information
  - o Sensitivity Analysis
    - ✓ "What if" analysis
    - ✓ Example
  - o Decision Tree Analysis
Example

- ❖ **Risk Management Software**
  - o Cost Risk Analysis
  - o Schedule Risk Analysis

- ❖ **Contingency**
  - o Contingency derived from a well-executed risk analysis could be a powerful project control tool.

Check on Learning

1. Cost variance greater than 20% is an example of a:

    A. Risk trigger
    B. Contingency allowance
    C. Active risk acceptance
    D. Management reserve

2. As part of your risk identification process, you feel one possible risk is the departure of a key team member who has special expertise that you need for your project. This is a:

    A. Source of risk
    B. Potential risk event
    C. Trigger
    D. Business risk

3. Project risk management includes all of the following except:

    A. Risk recognition through currency hedging
    B. Risk response development
    C. Risk identification
    D. Risk assessment

4. A possible risk is a computer virus. This is considered:

    A. An event
    B. The impact of an event
    C. The amount at stake
    D. A response

5. An input to risk identification is:

    A. Product description
    B. Historical Information
    C. Stakeholder risk tolerance
    D. Simulation

6. Your project calls for the development of new technology. At the end of the project, you will strive to obtain a patent. There is a 50% chance the patent will be granted, and a 50% chance that it will not be granted. This is an example of:

    A. Specifying the probability as a discrete function for decision tree analysis
    B. Specifying the outcome as a continuous function for decision tree analysis
    C. Providing a range of results for the probability and outcome
    D. A source of risk

7. In risk analysis using decision trees, which of the following statements is correct?

    A. The option with the highest Expected Value of cost is most economical
    B. The option with the lowest Expected Value of cost is most economical
    C. Cost savings actualized with an option are not considered in Expected Value calculations
    D. Risk treatment plans are required to validate the decision tree diagram

8. Risk response development will use which of the following approaches?

    A. Corrective action
    B. Risk management plan
    C. Workarounds
    D. Acceptance

9. Reducing the expected monetary value of a risk event by reducing the probability of occurrence or the risk event value or both is called:

    A. Risk control
    B. Risk response control
    C. Risk amelioration
    D. Corrective action

10. Agreeing to deal with the consequences of a risk event should it occur is called:

    A. Risk control
    B. Risk acceptance
    C. Risk avoidance
    D. Corrective action

11. If you want to transfer as much risk as possible to your supplier or subcontractor on a project you should use a:

    A. Cost-plus contract
    B. Fixed-price contract
    C. Cost-reimbursable contract
    D. Cost-plus-award-fee contract

12. Risk identification should be done:

    A. Only while preparing the project plan
    B. Only before a project review or a client meeting
    C. On a regular basis throughout the project
    D. Solely when cost or schedule variances occur

13. Which of the following is not a risk identification tool or technique?

      A.   Sensitivity calculations
      B.   Historical information
      C.   Strengths, weaknesses, opportunities, and threats analysis
      D.   Interviews

14. An information-gathering technique that is not used in risk identification is:

      A.   Questionnaire surveys
      B.   Expert Opinion
      C.   Brainstorming
      D.   Development of Risk Management Plans

15. Which of the following is not a primary risk component?

      A.   An event
      B.   The impact of the event
      C.   Probability of occurrence of the event
      D.   Expected monetary value of the event

Solutions

1.   A   Risk trigger
     Refer to Chapter 31, Internal and External Risks in Table 31.4

2.   B   Potential risk event
     Refer to Chapter 31, "Risk Identification" topic

3.   A   Risk recognition through currency hedging
     Refer to Chapter 31, "Fundamental Approach to Risk Management" topic

4.   A   An event
     Refer to Chapter 31, "Risk Identification" topic

5.   B   Historical Information
     Refer to Chapter 31, "Risk Identification" topic

6.   A   Specifying the probability as a discrete function for decision tree analysis
     Refer to Chapter 31, "Decision Tree Analysis" topic

7.   B   The option with the lowest Expected Value of cost is most economical
     Refer to Chapter 31, "Decision Tree Analysis" topic

8.   D   Acceptance
     Refer to Chapter 31, "Risk Control" topic

9.   A   Risk control
     Refer to Chapter 31, Risk Control" topic

10. B   Risk acceptance
     Refer to Chapter 31, "Risk Control" topic

11. B   Fixed-price contract
     Refer to Chapter 31, "Risk Control & Chapter 23 "Types of contracts" topics

12. C   On a regular basis throughout the project
     Refer to Chapter 31, "Risk Identification" topic

13. A   Sensitivity calculations
     Refer to Chapter 31, "Risk Identification" topic

14. D   Development of Risk Management Plans
     Refer to Chapter 31, "Risk Identification" topic

15. D   Expected monetary value of the event
     Refer to Chapter 31, "Risk Identification" topic

Chapter 32 – Risk Management Practical Guide

Allen C. Hamilton, PMP CCP

Introduction/Learning Objectives

Risk Management Practical Guide builds and expands on the principles outlined in Risk Management Fundamentals (Chapter 31). The chapter provides a practical "how to" guide on risk management. Of particular importance is the planning for and conducting risk management workshops, the utilization of Monte Carlo Simulation (MCS) workshops, and associated interviews. Contingency determination (i.e. using MCS) needs to fully address the potential impacts of project risks identified in the risk management plan. A well-managed risk management closure would benefit future projects with a higher degree of success. The key learning objectives are:

- Understand risk management.
- Identify the detailed steps of identifying risk, assessing risk occurrence and impact, and analyzing risk.
- Understand how to conduct a risk management work shop.
- Identify the key elements of conducting a Monte Carlo Simulation workshop.
- Describe the practical steps of risk treatment and risk control.
- Understand risk management close out and benefits to future projects.

Terms to Know

- Contingency
- Monte Carlo Simulation
- Risk Assessment &Treatment Threshold Matrix
- Risk Coding
- Risk Management Closure
- Risk Management Process
- Workshops – Risk & Monte Carlo Simulation

Key Points for Review

❖ **Risk Planning**
  o Objectives
  o Risk management team & organization
  o Risk management methods & tools
  o Use of TCM risk management process map

❖ **Risk Assessment**
  o Threats & opportunities identification
  o Risk register
  o Qualitative vs. quantitative analysis
  o Risk assessment & threat threshold matrix

- ❖ **Risk & Monte Carlo Simulation Workshops**
  - o Workshop Planning
    - ✓ Moderator internal vs. external
    - ✓ Workshop setting
    - ✓ Workshop participants matrix
  - o Conducting Workshops
    - ✓ Developing issues
    - ✓ Risk item coding
    - ✓ Identification & qualitative assessment
  - o Workshop Results
    - ✓ Workshop pitfalls
    - ✓ Analysis & results
    - ✓ Reporting & follow-up

- ❖ **Contingency**
  - o Inclusions vs. exclusions
  - o Contingency calculation methods

- ❖ **Monte Carlo Simulation (MCS)**
  - o Benefits & drawbacks
  - o Preparation & conducting MCS meeting
  - o Analysis & result presentation/communication

- ❖ **Risk Treatment**
  - o Key treatment actions
  - o Response strategies for threats
    - ✓ Avoid
    - ✓ Reduce
    - ✓ Transfer
    - ✓ Accept
  - o Response strategies for opportunities
    - ✓ Exploit
    - ✓ Share
    - ✓ Enhance
    - ✓ Accept

- ❖ **Risk Control**
  - o Response options
    - ✓ Act on risk
    - ✓ Modify risk
    - ✓ New risks

- ❖ **Risk Management Closure**
  - o Collect & debrief
  - o Evaluate & document
  - o Archive

Check on Learning

1. According to the TCM Process Map for Risk Management what are the four key steps?

    A. Risk planning, risk identification & risk analysis & risk treatment
    B. Risk planning, risk assessment, risk analysis & risk control
    C. Risk identification, risk assessment, risk treatment & risk control
    D. Risk planning, risk assessment, risk treatment & risk control

2. With respect to Risk Planning, what is the false statement below:

    A. A plan written during project development is the best approach
    B. The risk management plan will support the business goals and project objectives
    C. Methods and tools are fixed and should not be changed
    D. Considerations should be made to identify the formation of the risk management team

3. Risk assessment identification should include:

    A. Threats
    B. Opportunities
    C. Risks
    D. Threats & opportunities

4. With respect to Risk Assessment Analysis, identify a false statement from below:

    A. Considerations should be made to identify the formation of the risk management team
    B. Risk management of small projects may benefit from a three point scale
    C. Qualitative risk analysis is the assignment of subjective values to risk management items
    D. Risk assessment scores should receive appropriate analysis after the conclusion of the identification meetings if there is a question of accuracy

5. Risk Assessment & Treatment Threshold Matrix

    A. Is a way of keeping score for the risk workshop
    B. Is a technique to classifying risk issues for monitoring, potential treatment or definite treatment
    C. Only includes treats and excludes opportunities
    D. Includes opportunities & excludes threats

6. With respect to Risk Workshop Planning, identify the false statement below:

    A. Planning a risk management workshop should be consistent with the overall planning both for the project and risk management
    B. Smaller, less complex projects may justify a five day workshop conducted by a third party consultant
    C. Risk workshops should take place at the consultant's office
    D. Planning for the risk workshop should be completed after the start of the workshop

7. External workshop moderators have all the following advantages except:

    A. Big projects justify an external moderator
    B. External moderators can be objective in the implementation of the risk workshop
    C. External moderators are a member of the project team
    D. External moderators are in a better position to perform workshop follow-up

8. Monte Carlo work shop participants:

    A. Should be chosen at random from the project staff
    B. Should be appropriate to the development of project
    C. Should be all project staff
    D. Should be only high level managers

9. A common pitfall in Monte Carlo workshops with respect to the range selection of each cost group is:

    A. Selecting the highest but not the lowest range
    B. Selecting a range too low
    C. Selecting a range too narrow
    D. Selecting a range too low & too narrow

Solutions

1. D   Risk planning, risk assessment, risk treatment & risk control
   Refer to Chapter 32, Figure 32.1

2. C   Methods and tools are fixed and should not be changed
   Refer to Chapter 32, "Risk Planning" topic

3. D   Threats & opportunities
   Refer to Chapter 32, "Risk Assessment – Identification" topic

4. A   Considerations should be made to identify the formation of the risk management team
   Refer to Chapter 32, "Risk Assessment – Analysis, Qualitative Risk Analysis" topic

5. B   Is a technique to classifying risk issues for monitoring, potential treatment or definite treatment
   Refer to Chapter 32, "Risk Assessment Analysis, Qualitative Risk Analysis" topic

6. B   Smaller, less complex projects may justify a half day workshop conducted by a staff member.
   Refer to Chapter 32, "Risk workshop planning" topic

7. C   External moderators can be third party consultants or members of another company group not directly involved in the project implementation.
   Refer to Chapter 32, "Workshop Moderator Internal or External" topic

8. B   Workshop participants should be appropriate to the development stage of the project as shown in Table 2 MCS Participants by Type of Estimate.
   Refer to Chapter 32, Fig. 32.2

9. D   It has been demonstrated that project groups tend to show "group think" by selecting both low and narrow ranges.
   Refer to Chapter 32, "Benefits and Drawbacks - MCS" topic

Chapter 33 – Total Cost Management Overview

Larry R. Dysert, CCP CEP DRMP FAACE AACE Hon. Life

Introduction/Learning Objectives

Total Cost Management (TCM) is described as the "sum of the practices and processes that an enterprise uses to manage the total lifecycle cost investment in its portfolio of strategic assets". This study guide chapter will provide a basic understanding of the TCM Framework, allowing practitioners to understand how TCM is applied throughout the lifecycle of a given project or an enterprise. The key learning objectives are:

- Understand the project lifecycle.
- Understand how TCM is applied throughout the lifecycle of an asset
- Utilize the process map guides in the *TCM Framework*.
- Understand the Plan, Do, Check, Act (PDCA) management cycle.
- Understand the Strategic Asset Management Process and associate process map.
- Understand the Project Control Process and associate process map.

Terms to Know

- Ideation
- Plan-Do-Check-Act (PDCA) Management Cycle
- Process Map
- Strategic Asset
- Strategic Asset Management (SAM)
- TCM Framework
- Total Cost Management (TCM)

Key Points for Review

TCM attempts to illustrate the integration of all the various skills and knowledge areas that are required for processes to support overall management of both strategic assets as well as the individual projects, undertaken to create and develop those assets.

- ❖ **TCM is accomplished** through the application of:
  - ○ cost engineering and cost management principles
  - ○ proven methodologies
  - ○ the latest technologies in support of the management process

- ❖ **Strategic Assets** are physical or intellectual property that has long-term or lasting value to an enterprise. Additionally, they are expected to provide a positive economic benefit and are created through the investment of money, time, and resources. Examples include:
  - ○ buildings
  - ○ software applications
  - ○ retail products

o   theater production

It is important to note that TCM recognizes the term "cost" as going beyond the traditional monetary definition to include any investment of resources in the enterprise's assets. TCM is a comprehensive approach to managing the total resource investment in assets.

❖ **AACE International's Total Cost Management Framework: An Integrated Approach to Portfolio, Program, and Project Management**

The *TCM Framework* is AACE International's landmark technical publication that describes the concepts of total cost management. These principles are expressed within the framework as a series of process map guides that illustrate the highly integrated matrix of cost engineering and other business and management practices that support the lifecycle of asset investments. Simply stated, TCM is a systematic approach to managing cost throughout the lifecycle of an enterprise, program, facility, project, product, or service.

❖ **Total Cost Management Processes**
   o   Plan-Do-Check-Act (PDCA) Management Cycle
       ✓   Often referred to as the Deming or Shewhart Cycle
       ✓   Generally accepted, quality driven, continuous improvement model

The AACE International Total Cost Management process is divided into two (2) aspects:
1. **Strategic Asset Management (SAM) Process** (Fig. 33.2 & 33.4),
This refers to the macro process of managing the total lifecycle cost investment of resources in an enterprise's complete portfolio of strategic assets. This process focuses on initiating and managing the overall portfolio of projects in a way that addresses the strategic objectives of the enterprise. This process is typically business-led.

❖ **The lifecycle of a strategic asset** can be summarized by the following five (5) stages:
   o   **Ideation** – Determine an opportunity for a new asset; research, evaluate, define and develop potential solutions; select the optimal solution
   o   **Creation** – Create or implement the asset solution
   o   **Operation** – Deploy the new asset into service or operation
   o   **Modification** – Modify, improve or otherwise change the asset
   o   **Termination** – Decommission, retire, demolish or otherwise terminate the asset from the enterprise portfolio

❖ **The lifecycle of a project** can be summarized by the following four (4) phases:
   o   **Ideation** – Establish the project requirements and project goals
   o   **Planning** – Develop plans to achieve project requirements and goals
   o   **Execution** – Implement the project plans and execute the project to meet requirements and project goals
   o   **Closure** – Review, test, validate

Both lifecycles are illustrated within TCM to show the cyclical nature of the PDCA control steps. The sequence, depicted as a spiral, attempts to show that the process is employed continually to achieve various milestones at each stage or phase of the respective lifecycle.

2. Project Control Process (Fig. 33.2 & 33.5)

This is a technical-led a process for controlling the investment of resources in an asset during project execution. Project Control is the recursive process nested within the "DO" step of the Strategic Asset Management (SAM) Process cycle. Unlike SAM, which is always ongoing, a project is a temporary undertaking with a defined beginning and an end. Projects are how asset investment decisions are put into effect. Ultimately, at the end of a project, a usable or operational asset is returned to the enterprise's asset portfolio. Project Control is focused on delivering an asset that meets all of the business objectives identified by the strategic asset planning process; it is about "doing the project right".

Check on Learning

1. The TCM Framework identifies the P-D-C-A process steps as:

    A. Prepare, Decide, Collaborate, Act
    B. Plan, Do, Check, Act
    C. Propose, Determine, Communicate, Abate
    D. Plan, Do, Check, Assess

2. The five (5) steps of the project lifecycle include:

    A. Ideation, Planning, Execution & Closure
    B. Ideation, Creation, Operation, Modification & Termination
    C. There are only four (4) steps in the project lifecycle
    D. None of the above

3. Which TCM process focuses on initiating and managing the overall portfolio of projects in a way that addresses the strategic objectives of the enterprise?

    A. Project Control Process
    B. P-D-C-A Process
    C. Strategic Asset Management Process
    D. Total Cost Management Process

4. Which is NOT identified as a phase in the lifecycle of a project?

    A. Execution
    B. Planning
    C. Closure
    D. Initiation

5. Within the Strategic Asset Management Process, business management should continually be evaluating the asset portfolio to decide whether...

    A. A new asset should be developed
    B. An existing asset should be retired or decommissioned
    C. An existing asset should be modified
    D. All of the above

Fill in the blanks in the following sentence:

6. Project Controls is a _____ process nested within the _____ step of the Strategic Asset Management (SAM) cycle.

    A. Iterative, Plan
    B. Recursive, Do
    C. Repetitive, Assess

D. Useless, 3rd

7. Which process is illustrated as a spiral and shows how the process is employed continually throughout the lifecycle?

   A. Strategic Asset Management process
   B. P-D-C-A process
   C. Project Control process
   D. None of the above

8. _____ are temporary endeavors for the ideation, planning, execution, and closure of an asset.

   A. Assets
   B. Lemurs
   C. Employees
   D. Projects

9. The final stage in the lifecycle of a strategic asset is summarized as:

   A. Decommissioning – remove asset from service
   B. Modification – Improve or change asset
   C. Termination – Retire, demolish, or otherwise remove the asset
   D. None of the above

10. At which point in the SAM process does the transition from strategic asset management to project controls take place?

    A. Process Step (4.1), project implementation
    B. Process Step (5.2), asset performance measurement
    C. Process Step (3.1), requirements elicitation and analysis
    D. Process Step (6.1), asset performance assessment

Solutions

1.   B   Plan, Do, Check, Act
           Refer to Chapter 33, "Total Cost Management is a Process" topic

2.   C   There are only four (4) steps in the project lifecycle
           Refer to Chapter 33, "Total Cost Management is a Process" & Figure 33.3

3.   C   Strategic Asset Management Process
           Refer to Chapter 33, "Total Cost Management is a Process" topic

4.   D   Initiation
           Refer to Chapter 33, "Total Cost Management is a Process" topic

5.   D   All of the above
           Refer to Chapter 33, "The Strategic Asset Management Process" topic

6.   B   Recursive, Do
           Refer to Chapter 33, "The Project Control Process" topic

7.   B   P-D-C-A process
           Refer to Chapter 33, "Total Cost Management is a Process" topic & Figure 33.3

8.   D   Projects
           Refer to Chapter 33, "Total Cost Management is a Process" topic

9.   C   Termination – Retire, demolish, or otherwise remove the asset
           Refer to Chapter 33, "Total Cost Management is a Process" topic

10.   A   Process Step (4.1), project implementation
           Refer to Chapter 33, "The Strategic Asset Management Process" topic & Figures 33.2; 33.4

Chapter 34 – The International System of Units (SI)

Kurt G. R. Heinze, P.Eng. ECCP FAACE AACE Hon. Life

Introduction/Learning Objectives

The Système International d'Unites (The international system of units), also known as (SI), was adopted in 1960 to facilitate the world market outreach. When working on multi-national projects and contracts, familiarity of SI is essential to improve project controls and communication. The key learning objectives of this chapter are:

- Identify the seven base SI units of measurement.
- Understand the unit conversions from SI to non-SI units and vice versa.
- Understand the rules for SI style and usage to be able to properly express units.

Terms to Know

- Base Units
- Conversion Factors
- Derived Units
- Hard Conversion
- Metric Conversion
- SI
- Significant Digits
- Soft Conversion

Key Points for Review

- ❖ **SI**: The international system of units
- ❖ **Metric conversion**: Changeover from the U.S. customary measuring system to the SI
- ❖ **Soft conversion**: Calculated equivalent of the customary measuring expressions in metric terms
- ❖ **Hard conversion**: A complete immersion into the new "language" and applications of the SI without reference to the old system and the opportunity to review old standards
- ❖ **Significant digits**: When conversion calculations are performed, accuracy of the original data should be taken into account

Check on Learning

1. You are preparing an international bid and need to convert existing database to SI unit. The current unit labor rate is 2 WH/ft to install 10" SS pipe. Which one of the following is the closest conversion to install 25 cm SS pipe before making location factor adjustment:

    A. 6.67 WH/m
    B. 6.56 WH/m
    C. 0.66 WH/m
    D. None of the above

2. If it takes 8 WH/cy to pour concrete foundation, what is the equivalent WH/m^3:

    A. 6.08 WH/ m^3
    B. 7.32 WH/ m^3
    C. 10.5 WH/ m^3
    D. None of the above

3. The job site temperature recorded is 25 °C. What is the equivalent °F?

    A. 45 °F
    B. 77 °F
    C. 57 °F
    D. None of the above

4. You are performing bid evaluation of four bidders based on fabricating 20" (50 cm) diameter 304L SS straight pipe section. Which one the following has the highest unit price?

    A. $144/ft
    B. $460/m
    C. $378/m
    D. $176/ft

5. A 40 ft container has a net shipping weight of 54 000 kg. What is equivalent ton?

    A. 53.2 ton (long)
    B. 60 ton (short)
    C. 54 ton
    D. All of the above

6. The engineering pump specifications call for a water pump with a minimum discharge pressure of 1000 psi (lb/inch^2). You need to source pump in Malaysia. What is the minimum acceptable pump discharge pressure?

    A. 6 894 kPa (kilopascal)
    B. 6 800 kPa
    C. 7 000 kPa
    D. 7 100 kPa

7. You have recently completed a 200,000 ft² warehouse construction. A potential client in Chile is interested in the same warehouse size. How would you describe your proposed warehouse size?

    A.   18 000 m²
    B.   18 600 m²
    C.   19 000 m²
    D.   20 000 m²

8. Unleaded gas is available at the following four gas stations. Which one offers the most attractive gas price?

    A. $3.35/G (US)
    B. $4.15/G (Canada)
    C. $1.05/L
    D.   Not enough information to determine

9. Your US Headquarters is committed to reduce energy consumption by setting office summer temperature at 70 °F. What is the recommended temperature in °C?

    A.   38.9 °C
    B.   21.1 °C
    C.   23 °C
    D.   Not enough information to determine

10. Your crew is erecting a 40 ft power pole. What is the equivalent pole length in SI unit?

    A.   11.8 m
    B.   12 m
    C.   12.2 m
    D.   Not enough information to determine

Solutions

1. B   Based on 1 ft = 0.3048 m conversion factor
         2 WH/ft = 2 WH/0.3048 m = **6.56 WH/m**

2. C   Based on 1 yard = 0.9144 m → 1 cy = $(0.9144)^3$ m^3= 0.76 m^3
         8 WH/cy = 8 WH/0.76 m^3 = **10.5 m^3**

3. B   Use °F = (9/5)°C + 32
         (9/5)*25+32 = **77°F**

4. D   Use 1 ft = 0.3048 m factor to convert unit prices from per ft to per meter
         $144/ft = $144/0.3048 m = $472/m
         $176/ft = $176/0.3048 m = $577/m (The highest unit price)

5. A   Based on 1 ton (long) = 1016 kg → 54 000 kg/1016 kg = **53.2 ton (long)**
         Based on 1 ton (short) = 907 kg → 54 000 kg/907 kg = 59.5 ton (short)

6. A   Based on 1 psi (lb/inch2) = 6 894 pascal (Pa)
         1 000 psi = 1 000 X 6 894 Pa = 6 894 000 Pa = **6 894 kPa**

7. B   Based on 1 ft = 0.3048 m → 1 ft^2 = $(0.3048$ m$)^2$ m^2 = 0.0929 m^2
         200 000 ft^2 = 200 000 ft^2 X 0.0929 m^2/ ft^2 = 18 580 m^2
         Round the answer to **18 600 m^2** (Approximate 186 m X 100 m warehouse)

8. A   Based on 1 Gallon (US) = 3.785 L → $3.35 /G (US) = $3.35/G ÷ 3.785 L/G = $0.89 /L
         Based on 1 Gallon (Canada) = 4.546 L → $4.15 /G (Canada)
                                    = $4.15/G ÷ 4.546 L/G = $0.91 /L
         $3.35/G (US) has the lowest unit cost

9. B   Use °C = (5/9)*(°F – 32)
         (5/9)*(70 – 32) = 21.1 °C

10. C   Based on 1 ft = 0.3048 m conversion factor
         40 ft X 0.3048 m/ft = **12.2 m**

APPENDICES

APPENDIX A – Sample Exam Questions

Items 1 – 5 are compound practice exercises with a number of questions pertaining to each exercise.

1. An engineering company was awarded a project with an original budget of 160,000 hours, valued at $15,000,000. The Client has asked the project team to prepare an in-depth analysis of the project performance and make a formal presentation.

Use the following data to prepare the reports and presentation as requested by the Client.

- Planned hours: 65,000
- Actual hours spent to date: 73,000
- % complete: 40%

1a. How many hours has the project earned?

    A. 64,000
    B. 73,000
    C. 6,400
    D. 5,900

1b. What is the cost variance (CV)?

    A. -9,000
    B. +8,000
    C. -12,000
    D. +7,000

1c. What is the schedule variance (SV)?

    A. -1,000
    B. +1,000
    C. -9,000
    D. +10,000

1d. What is the cost performance index (CPI)?

    A. .88
    B. 1.14
    C. .98
    D. .89

1e. What is the schedule performance index (SPI)?

    A. .98
    B. 1.01
    C. .89
    D. 1.25

1f. What are the forecasted work hours to complete (EAC)?

    A. 181,818
    B. 169,000
    C. 160,000
    D. 183,890

1g. What is the status of the project?

    A. Cost favorable, Schedule unfavorable
    B. Cost favorable, Schedule favorable
    C. Schedule unfavorable, Cost unfavorable
    D. Schedule unfavorable, Cost favorable

2. It is necessary to perform operating and manufacturing cost estimates at both full plant capacity and at conditions other than full plant capacity. An analysis of costs at other than full plan capacity needs to take into account fixed, variable, and semi-variable costs. Answer the following seven (7) questions relating to this scenario.

2a. An analysis of operating and maintenance costs at partial capacity enables the determination of:

    A. Variable costs
    B. Fixed costs
    C. Semi-variable costs
    D. Break-even point

2b. Those costs that are independent of the system throughput are:

    A. Variable costs
    B. Fixed costs
    C. Operating costs
    D. All of the above

2c. Semi-variable costs could include:

    A. Costs that are not directly fixed
    B. Supervision
    C. Plant overhead
    D. All of the above

2d. Fixed costs include all of the following except:

    A. Depreciation
    B. Property taxes
    C. Utilities
    D. All of the above

2e. What is another name for semi-variable costs?

    A. Proportional costs
    B. Production costs
    C. Manufacturing costs
    D. Packaging costs

2f. Royalty cost can be considered as:

    A. Variable costs
    B. Semi-variable costs
    C. Fixed costs
    D. Any of the above

2g. Which of the following is an example of a fixed cost?

    A. Depreciation
    B. General expense
    C. Plant overhead
    D. Material

3. A construction contractor borrows $50,000 to take advantage of a 2% cash discount offered on material required for the project. The note is a single note payable in 60 days at an 11% annual interest rate (assumed 365 days). However, the contractor receives construction progress payments and applies part of the note as follows:

$20,000 paid on the note 15 days after the note is made.
$20,000 paid 30 days from the date of the original note.
$10,000 balance paid on the maturity date of 60 days.

Assumption: With simple interest, single payment notes, any amount paid on the principal stops the interest paid on that amount as of the date payment is made.

To work this problem you will need to find the total amount of interest paid, how much money the contractor saved by making partial payments on the note, and the percent saved. Use 4 decimal places for all calculations. Answer the following seven (7) questions regarding this scenario.

3a. What is the total amount of interest paid?

    A. $452.10
    B. $451.00
    C. $904.20
    D. $902.00

3b. How much did the contractor save by making partial payments on the note?

    A. $451.00
    B. $452.10
    C. $226.05
    D. $225.50

3c. The total amount of interest due in 60 days with no partial payments on the note is:

    A. $904.20
    B. $656.00
    C. $657.60
    D. $902.00

3d. What is the percent saved?

    A. 1.8%
    B. 25%
    C. 50%
    D. 24.9%

3e. The significance of the assumption in the calculation of this problem is:

    A. Compounding of interest is avoided by making partial payments
    B. The present value of the loan is minimized
    C. The loan can be depreciated earlier by making partial payments
    D. The amount of savings can be increased by the partial payments

3f. If the contractor actually paid $50,000 for job material, how much did he save by taking the cash discount?

    A. $1,000.24
    B. $2,000.60
    C. $1,200.03
    D. $1,020.41

3g. The total saved in interest plus the cash discount is:

    A. $1,472.51
    B. $1,451.00
    C. $1,426.05
    D. $2,225.50

4. ABC Valve Company is purchasing a sub-component part from a vendor and is experiencing quality difficulties. Ten percent (10%) of the parts have been defective and rejected. Reworking the part and scrap has averaged $16 per component. Projected sales over the next two (2) years indicate that 4,000 parts will be required for manufacturing the valves. Engineering has suggested and defined two methods to reduce the risk of questionable parts. Cost of the part will only be borne by the vendor if the parts are rejected upon delivery. Therefore, engineering is proposing either a visual or gauged inspection upon receipt.

Visual inspection would reduce the receipt of defective sub-components by 5%. Labor cost for visual inspection would be $1,000 per year.

If gauges for testing were purchased for $1,800, receipt of defective sub-components would drop to 0.5%. Annual Labor cost for gauged inspections would be $1,700 with a one-time training cost of $600.

Ignore the impact of interest and escalation for the estimated costs. Answer the following 7 questions regarding this scenario.

4a. The number of defective components for no inspection, gauged, and visual is:

    A. 200,20,400
    B. 100,10,200
    C. 400,20,200
    D. 200,100,10

4b. What is the cost of the gauged inspections not counting rework?

    A. $4,100
    B. $5,800
    C. $6,120
    D. None of the above

4c. What is the total cost if no inspections are performed?

    A. $1,640
    B. $2,640
    C. $6,400
    D. None of the above

4d. What is the total cost if gauged inspections are selected?

    A. $5,800
    B. $6,120
    C. $4,420
    D. None of the above

4e. What is the total cost if visual inspections are selected?

    A. $4,200
    B. $1,600
    C. $5,000
    D. $5,200

4f. What inspection recommendation would you suggest to management?

    A. No inspection
    B. Gauged inspection
    C. Visual inspection
    D. Combination of visual and gauged inspection

4g. If used gauges could be purchased for $1,000, what inspection method would you recommend?

    A. No inspection
    B. Gauged inspection
    C. Visual inspection
    D. Combination of visual and gauged inspection

5. You are AACE International certified Project Manager on a large long term project with over 200 personnel under your leadership. The project was under funded from the start and problems have developed with schedule slips. Consequently, morale is not the best. Answer the following seven (7) questions regarding communication and ethics.

5a. Which of the following is not an essential attribute for communicating with the project personnel?

    A. Your knowledge and understanding of human motives
    B. Your ability to be respected and trusted by peers
    C. Your proficiency with the art of persuasion
    D. Your ability to avoid answering tough questions

5b. The following should all be considered before initiating a communication except:

    A. The purpose of the communication
    B. Is the message valid for tomorrow as well as today?
    C. Do your everyday actions support your words?
    D. None of the above

5c. A trade magazine has asked for information to publish a story of the project. Which of the following should not be a guideline for information supplied?

    A. Remain dignified and modest during any interviews
    B. Statements should be objective and truthful
    C. Seek acknowledgement for yourself, and AACE
    D. Only supply information for which you are qualified

5d. Which of the following statements or actions cannot inhibit communications?

    A. Giving insincere praise
    B. Treating a serious problem, seriously
    C. Telling the other person what to do
    D. Psychoanalyzing the other person

5e. Which of the following guidelines does not apply to written communication?

    A. Use complete sentences that are short, with short words
    B. Limit each paragraph to a primary and secondary idea
    C. Avoid use of jargon and abbreviations in the document
    D. Have a beginning, middle, and end to the document

5f. The best way to improve your verbal and written communication effectiveness is:

    A. Actual practice
    B. Reading technical papers
    C. Video training
    D. Professional assistance

5g. Which of the following is not generally true of successful meetings?

    A. Meetings should start and end on schedule
    B. Meetings require preparation, and control
    C. Time should be allowed for extraneous discussion
    D. Minutes are taken and distributed to the attendees

Part B:

Answer all of the following Part B questions. Select only one answer per question. If you select more than one answer per question the question will be marked incorrect.

1. As the purchasing manager for a local company located in the USA, you receive a request from a purchasing manager representing a project buyer overseas for a price quotation for six (6) kilograms (kg) of Babbitt for a project. Babbitt is priced in your firm for $3.62 per pound. What price would you quote (in US dollars excluding freight) in reply to the request?

     A. $47.88
     B. $21.72
     C. $ 4.78
     D. $27.15

2. The following technique can be used to prepare an Order of Magnitude estimate:

     A. Parametric Estimate
     B. Monte Carlo Method
     C. Detailed Takeoffs and Pricing
     D. All of the above

3. Which condition listed below would not enable Liquidated Damages to be applied to a contract?

     A. Delay in the completion of the overall contract
     B. Loss of revenue for the owner
     C. Acts of nature
     D. Unreasonable inconvenience

4. A method of evaluating project or investments by comparing the present value or annual value of expected benefits to the present value or annual value of expected costs is referred to as:

     A. Benefit Cost Analysis
     B. Net Present Value
     C. Rate of Return
     D. Buy Back Analysis

5. If you buy a set of baseball cards for $60.00 and sell them 4 years later for $90.00, what is the annual rate of return?

     A. 9.5%
     B. 10.7%
     C. 11.4%
     D. 12.3%

6. The formula for Schedule Variance (SV) is:

    A. BCWP / BCWS
    B. BCWP – BCWS
    C. BCWP – ACWP
    D. BCWS - BCWP

7. The formula for Schedule Performance Index (SPI) is:

    A. BCWP / BCWS
    B. BCWP / ACWP
    C. BCWS / BCWP
    D. BCWS / ACWP

8. Resources that are expended solely to complete the activity or asset is called:

    A. Direct Costs
    B. Indirect Costs
    C. Fixed Costs
    D. Variable Costs

9. ABC Computer Company assembles computers in the Atlanta area. Each fully assembled computer sells for $1,200, it costs ABC Computer Co. $700 to assemble each computer and ready for shipping. The fixed costs for ABC Computer Co. are $1,500. What is the break-even point in units for ABC Computer?

    A. 3
    B. 6
    C. 2
    D. 4

10. Design Basis, Planning Basis, Cost Basis, and Risk Basis are all clearly defined in what document?

    A. Estimating Department Guidelines (EDG)
    B. Contingency and Risk Analysis (C&RA)
    C. Basis of Estimate (BOE)
    D. Design Readiness Review (DRR)

11. Influencing the future by making decision based on missions, needs, and objectives is the definition for:

    A. Planning
    B. Scheduling
    C. Estimating
    D. Cost Reporting

12. The _____ through the network determines each activity's ES and EF and the project's duration or the earliest date a project can finish.

    A. Backward Pass
    B. Coding Techniques
    C. Forward Pass
    D. Time-scaled logic diagrams

13. The most complex form of organization structure is the _____ organization.

    A. Functional
    B. Departmental
    C. Matrix
    D. Product-line

14. A Project Controls Professional from Alberta Canada relocates to a job site in south Texas. Upon arrival in Texas, the temperature was recorded at 85 degrees Fahrenheit. Since our Project Controls Professional is accustom to reading temperatures in Celsius, what would the temperature be in degrees Celsius?

    A. 29
    B. 95
    C. 45
    D. 19

15. To _____ another is to protect them against loss or damage either by paying for the loss or standing in their place in the event of a legal dispute.

    A. Insure
    B. Indemnify
    C. Force Majeure
    D. Audit

16. The two fundamental approaches to cash flow analysis are:

    A. Equivalent Worth, Rate of Return
    B. Benefit-Cost Ratio, Present Worth
    C. Future Value, Net Future Worth
    D. Capitalized Cost, Depreciation

17. _____ is a formal lawsuit in a state or federal court pursuant to the terms of the contract and under the rules of the jurisdiction where the lawsuit is filed.

    A. Mediation
    B. Litigation
    C. Arbitration
    D. Liability

18. According to AACE International RP 17R-97, Cost Estimate Classification, the purpose of a Class 3 estimate is:

    A. Control or Bid Tender
    B. Budget Authorization
    C. Conceptual Study
    D. Screening

19. _____ allows activities to be grouped together, which reduces the number of activities in a network and can reduce the overall time of performance.

    A. Overlapping network techniques
    B. Work breakdown structure
    C. Project evaluation review technique
    D. Activity coding techniques

ANSWERS AND SOLUTIONS:

PART A

A.1a.   A

            SOLUTION: Earned value = % complete X budget

                                       .40 X 160,000 = 64,000 hours earned

A.1b.   A

            SOLUTION: CV = BCWP - ACWP
                                       (earned hours – actual hours)

                                       64,000 – 73,000 = -9,000

A.1c.   A

            SOLUTION: SV = BCWP – BCWS
                                       (earned hours – planned hours)

                                       64,000 – 65,000 = -1,000

A.1d.   A

            SOLUTION: CPI = BCWP / ACWP
                                       (earned / actual)

                                       64,000 / 73,000 = .88

A.1e.   A

            SOLUTION: SPI = BCWP / BCWS
                                       (earned / planned)

                                       64,000 / 65,000 = .98

A.1f.   A

            SOLUTION: EAC = BAC / CPI
                                       160,000 / .88 = 181,818

A.1g.   C

          SOLUTION: Cost: CV = -9000 hours (over budget)
                                    CPI = .88 (below 1.0 reflects over budget)

                       Schedule: SV = -1,000 hours (slightly behind schedule)
                                    SPI = .98 (below 1.0 reflects behind planned)

                       Earned Hours: 64,000

                       Actual Hours Spent: 73,000   (spending too many hours and not earning
                                                      value on all the hours spent to date)

                       Original Budget: 160,000

                       Forecast at Complete: 181,818

ANSWER SOURCE: Skills & Knowledge 6, Chapters 14 and 15.

A.2a.   D
A.2b.   B
A.2c.   D
A.2d.   C
A.2e.   A
A.2f.   D
A.2g.   A

ANSWER SOURCE: Skills & Knowledge 6, Chapter 10

A.3a.   A

SOLUTION:

INTEREST = PRINCIPAL x RATE x TIME

1st $20,000
payment $50,000.00   X 11%   X (15/365)

                                                   (use 4 decimal places, round up on
               $50,000.00   X .11   X .0411   5th place if 5 or greater)

               $226.05

2nd $20,000
payment $50,000.00   minus 1st payment of $20,000 = $30,000

               $30,000.00   X 11%   X (15/365)

               $135.63

$10,000 final
payment $10,000.00   X 11%   X (30/365)

                                                   (use 4 decimal places, round up on
               $10,000.00   X .11   X .0822   5th place if 5 or greater)

               $90.42

               1ST PAYMENT + 2 PAYMENT + 3 PAYMENT

               $266.05 $135.63 $90.42

               | $ 452.10 |

A.3b.   B

SOLUTION:

INTEREST = P X R X T

$50,000.00   X 11%   X   (60/365)

                                              (Use 4 decimal places, round up on
$50,000.00   X .11   X   .1644   5th place if 5 or greater)

$904.20

$904.20   minus $ 452.10

$452.10

A.3c.   A

SOLUTION :

INTEREST = P X R X T

$50,000.00   X 11%   X   (60/365)

                                              (use 4 decimal places, round up on
$50,000.00   X .11   X   .1644   5th place if 5 or greater)

$904.20

A.3d.   C

SOLUTION:

$452.10   divided by $904.20

50%

A.3e.   D

A.3f.   D

SOLUTION: $50,000.00   Actually paid
                 2% or (1-.02)

                 $50,000 divided by .98

                 $51,020.41

                 $51,020.41 minus $50,000.00 = $1,020.41

A.3g.   A

SOLUTION: $ 1,020.41   saved by cash discount
                 $ 452.10   saved in interest
                 $ 1,472.51   total saved

A.4a.   C

SOLUTION:

No inspection   10% x 4000
                                          400

Gauged   .5% x 4000
                                           20

Visual   5% X 4000
                                          200

A.4b.   B

                                                        (reminder: labor for 2
SOLUTION: $ 1,800.00   + ($1700 x 2) + $600   years)
                       $ 5,800.00

A.4c.   C

SOLUTION: 10% x 4000 x $16.00
                       $ 6,400.00

276

A.4d.   B

SOLUTION:

0.5% x 4000 x $16.00

$ 320.00

$ 5,800.00   cost of gauged inspections, plus labor and training

$ 6,120.00

A.4e.   D

SOLUTION:

5% x 4000 x $16.00
$ 3,200.00
$ 2,000.00   (labor for 2 years)
$ 5,200.00

A.4f.   C

SOLUTION:

gauged $6,120.00

visual $5,200.00

no inspection $6,400.00

VISUAL INSPECTION -- MOST COST EFFICIENT

A.4g.   C

SOLUTION:

$ 1,000.00   + ($1700 x 2) + $600   (reminder: labor for 2 years)
$ 5,000.00

0.5% x 4000 x $16.00
$ 320.00
$ 5,000.00   cost of gauged inspections, plus labor and training
$ 5,320.00

VISUAL INSPECTION - STILL MORE COST EFFICIENT

ANSWER SOURCE: Skills & Knowledge 6, Chapter 6.

A.5a.	D
A.5b.	D
A.5c.	C
A.5d.	B
A.5e.	B
A.5f.	A
A.5g.	C

ANSWER SOURCE: Skills & Knowledge 6, Chapter 20.

PART B ANSWERS:

B.1   A

SOLUTION:
Convert kilograms to pounds
6 kilograms divided by .4535924 = 13.2278 pounds
13.2278 pounds X $3.62 / pound = $47.88 for order of Babbitt for this project

ANSWER SOURCE: Skills & Knowledge 6, Chapter 34.

B.2   A

ANSWER SOURCE: Skills & Knowledge 6, Chapter 9.

B.3   C

ANSWER SOURCE: Skills & Knowledge 6, Chapter 25.

B.4   A

ANSWER SOURCE: Skills & Knowledge 6, Chapter 7.

B.5　　　　　　　　　　B

SOLUTION:
$F = P (1 + i)^n$
$90 = 60 (1 + i)^4$
$90 / 60 = (1 + i)^4$
$1.5 = (1 + i)^4$
$i = 10.7\%$

ANSWER SOURCE: Skills & Knowledge 6, Chapter 27.

B.6　　　　　　　　　　B

ANSWER SOURCE: Skills & Knowledge 6, Chapter 14.

B.7　　　　　　　　　　A

ANSWER SOURCE: Skills & Knowledge 6, Chapter 14.

B.8　　　　　　　　　　A

ANSWER SOURCE: Skills & Knowledge 6, Chapter 1.

B.9　　　　　　　　　　A

SOLUTION:
Selling Price = $1,200
Variable Costs = $700
Fixed Costs = $1,500

$X = FC / (SP - VC)$
$X = \$1,500 / (\$1200 - \$700)$
$X = \$1,500 / \$500$
$X = 3$ units

ANSWER SOURCE: Skills & Knowledge 6, Chapter 2.

B.10　　　　　　　　　　C

ANSWER SOURCE: Skills & Knowledge 6, Chapter 9.

B.11　　　　　　　　　　A

ANSWER SOURCE: Skills & Knowledge 6, Chapter 12.

B.12   C

ANSWER SOURCE: Skills & Knowledge 6, Chapter 13.

B.13   C

ANSWER SOURCE: Skills & Knowledge 6, Chapter 17.

B.14   A

SOLUTION:
Convert degrees Fahrenheit to degrees Celsius
$(5 / 9) (F - 32) = C$
$.5556 (85 - 32) = C$
85 degrees F = 29 degrees C

ANSWER SOURCE: Skills & Knowledge 6, Chapter 34.

B.15   B

ANSWER SOURCE: Skills & Knowledge 6, Chapter 23.

B.16   A

ANSWER SOURCE: Skills & Knowledge 6, Chapter 27.

B.17   B

ANSWER SOURCE: Skills & Knowledge 6, Chapter 23.

B.18   B

ANSWER SOURCE: Skills & Knowledge 6, Chapter 9.

B.19   A

ANSWER SOURCE: Skills & Knowledge 6, Chapter 13.

APPENDIX B – Values of the Standard Normal Distribution Function

Z	0	1	2	3	4	5	6	7	8	9
-3.0	0.0013	0.0010	0.0007	0.0005	0.0003	0.0002	0.0002	0.0001	0.0001	0.0000
-2.9	0.0019	0.0018	0.0017	0.0017	0.0016	0.0016	0.0015	0.0015	0.0014	0.0014
-2.8	0.0026	0.0025	0.0024	0.0023	0.0023	0.0022	0.0021	0.0021	0.0020	0.0019
-2.7	0.0035	0.0034	0.0033	0.0032	0.0031	0.0030	0.0029	0.0028	0.0027	0.0026
-2.6	0.0047	0.0045	0.0044	0.0043	0.0041	0.0040	0.0039	0.0038	0.0037	0.0036
-2.5	0.0062	0.0060	0.0059	0.0057	0.0055	0.0054	0.0052	0.0051	0.0049	0.0048
-2.4	0.0082	0.0080	0.0078	0.0075	0.0073	0.0071	0.0069	0.0068	0.0066	0.0064
-2.3	0.0107	0.0104	0.0102	0.0099	0.0096	0.0094	0.0091	0.0089	0.0087	0.0084
-2.2	0.0139	0.0136	0.0132	0.0129	0.0126	0.0122	0.0119	0.0116	0.0113	0.0110
-2.1	0.0179	0.0174	0.0170	0.0166	0.0162	0.0158	0.0154	0.0150	0.0146	0.0143
-2.0	0.0228	0.0222	0.0217	0.0212	0.0207	0.0202	0.0197	0.0192	0.0188	0.0183
-1.9	0.0287	0.0281	0.0274	0.0268	0.0262	0.0256	0.0250	0.0244	0.0238	0.0233
-1.8	0.0359	0.0352	0.0344	0.0336	0.0329	0.0322	0.0314	0.0307	0.0300	0.0294
-1.7	0.0446	0.0436	0.0427	0.0418	0.0409	0.0401	0.0392	0.0384	0.0375	0.0367
-1.6	0.0548	0.0537	0.0526	0.0516	0.0505	0.0495	0.0485	0.0475	0.0465	0.0455
-1.5	0.0668	0.0655	0.0643	0.0630	0.0618	0.0606	0.0594	0.0582	0.0570	0.0559
-1.4	0.0808	0.0793	0.0778	0.0764	0.0749	0.0735	0.0722	0.0708	0.0694	0.0681
-1.3	0.0968	0.0951	0.0934	0.0918	0.0901	0.0885	0.0869	0.0853	0.0838	0.0823
-1.2	0.1151	0.1131	0.1112	0.1093	0.1075	0.1056	0.1038	0.1020	0.1003	0.0985
-1.1	0.1357	0.1335	0.1314	0.1292	0.1271	0.1251	0.1230	0.1210	0.1190	0.1170
-1.0	0.1587	0.1562	0.1539	0.1515	0.1492	0.1469	0.1446	0.1423	0.1401	0.1379
-0.9	0.1841	0.1814	0.1788	0.1762	0.1736	0.1711	0.1685	0.1660	0.1635	0.1611
-0.8	0.2119	0.2090	0.2061	0.2033	0.2005	0.1977	0.1949	0.1922	0.1894	0.1867
-0.7	0.2420	0.2389	0.2358	0.2327	0.2297	0.2266	0.2236	0.2206	0.2177	0.2148
-0.6	0.2743	0.2709	0.2676	0.2643	0.2611	0.2578	0.2546	0.2514	0.2483	0.2451
-0.5	0.3085	0.3050	0.3015	0.2981	0.2946	0.2912	0.2877	0.2843	0.2810	0.2776
-0.4	0.3446	0.3409	0.3372	0.3336	0.3300	0.3264	0.3228	0.3192	0.3156	0.3121
-0.3	0.3821	0.3783	0.3745	0.3707	0.3669	0.3632	0.3594	0.3557	0.3520	0.3483
-0.2	0.4207	0.4168	0.4129	0.4090	0.4052	0.4013	0.3974	0.3936	0.3897	0.3859
-0.1	0.4602	0.4562	0.4522	0.4483	0.4443	0.4404	0.4364	0.4325	0.4286	0.4247
-0.0	0.5000	0.4960	0.4920	0.4880	0.4840	0.4801	0.4761	0.4721	0.4681	0.4641

Z	0	1	2	3	4	5	6	7	8	9
0.0	0.5000	0.5040	0.5080	0.5120	0.5160	0.5199	0.5239	0.5279	0.5319	0.5359
0.1	0.5398	0.5438	0.5478	0.5517	0.5557	0.5596	0.5636	0.5675	0.5714	0.5753
0.2	0.5793	0.5832	0.5871	0.5910	0.5948	0.5987	0.6026	0.6064	0.6103	0.6141
0.3	0.6179	0.6217	0.6255	0.6293	0.6331	0.6368	0.6406	0.6443	0.6480	0.6517
0.4	0.6554	0.6591	0.6628	0.6664	0.6700	0.6736	0.6772	0.6808	0.6844	0.6879
0.5	0.6915	0.6950	0.6985	0.7019	0.7054	0.7088	0.7123	0.7157	0.7190	0.7224
0.6	0.7257	0.7291	0.7324	0.7357	0.7389	0.7422	0.7454	0.7486	0.7517	0.7549
0.7	0.7580	0.7611	0.7642	0.7673	0.7703	0.7734	0.7764	0.7794	0.7823	0.7852
0.8	0.7881	0.7910	0.7939	0.7967	0.7995	0.8023	0.8051	0.8078	0.8106	0.8133
0.9	0.8159	0.8186	0.8212	0.8238	0.8264	0.8289	0.8315	0.8340	0.8365	0.8389
1.0	0.8413	0.8438	0.8461	0.8485	0.8508	0.8531	0.8554	0.8577	0.8599	0.8621
1.1	0.8643	0.8665	0.8686	0.8708	0.8729	0.8749	0.8770	0.8790	0.8810	0.8830
1.2	0.8849	0.8869	0.8888	0.8907	0.8925	0.8944	0.8962	0.8980	0.8997	0.9015
1.3	0.9032	0.9049	0.9066	0.9082	0.9099	0.9115	0.9131	0.9147	0.9162	0.9177
1.4	0.9192	0.9207	0.9222	0.9236	0.9251	0.9265	0.9278	0.9292	0.9306	0.9319
1.5	0.9332	0.9345	0.9357	0.9370	0.9382	0.9394	0.9406	0.9418	0.9430	0.9441
1.6	0.9452	0.9463	0.9474	0.9484	0.9495	0.9505	0.9515	0.9525	0.9535	0.9545
1.7	0.9554	0.9564	0.9573	0.9582	0.9591	0.9599	0.9608	0.9616	0.9625	0.9633
1.8	0.9641	0.9648	0.9656	0.9664	0.9671	0.9678	0.9686	0.9693	0.9700	0.9706
1.9	0.9713	0.9719	0.9726	0.9732	0.9738	0.9744	0.9750	0.9756	0.9762	0.9767
2.0	0.9772	0.9778	0.9783	0.9788	0.9793	0.9798	0.9803	0.9808	0.9812	0.9817
2.1	0.9821	0.9826	0.9830	0.9834	0.9838	0.9842	0.9846	0.9850	0.9854	0.9857
2.2	0.9861	0.9864	0.9868	0.9871	0.9874	0.9878	0.9881	0.9884	0.9887	0.9890
2.3	0.9893	0.9896	0.9898	0.9901	0.9904	0.9906	0.9909	0.9911	0.9913	0.9916
2.4	0.9918	0.9920	0.9922	0.9925	0.9927	0.9929	0.9931	0.9932	0.9934	0.9936
2.5	0.9938	0.9940	0.9941	0.9943	0.9945	0.9946	0.9948	0.9949	0.9951	0.9952
2.6	0.9953	0.9955	0.9956	0.9957	0.9959	0.9960	0.9961	0.9962	0.9963	0.9964
2.7	0.9965	0.9966	0.9967	0.9968	0.9969	0.9970	0.9971	0.9972	0.9973	0.9974
2.8	0.9974	0.9975	0.9976	0.9977	0.9977	0.9978	0.9979	0.9979	0.9980	0.9981
2.9	0.9981	0.9982	0.9982	0.9983	0.9984	0.9984	0.9985	0.9985	0.9986	0.9986
3.0	0.9987	0.9990	0.9993	0.9995	0.9997	0.9998	0.9998	0.9999	0.9999	1.0000

APPENDIX C – Discrete Compound Interest Tables

SYMBOLS

The following symbols are used in the following tables:

A Periodic payment (i.e. Annual amount). A uniform series of end-of-period payments or receipts, $
F Future value, a single lump sum value occurring at the end of the last of n time periods, $
i Interest rate per period, decimal
n Total number of compounding periods, decimal
P Present value, a single lump sum occurring at time zero, the first of n time periods, $
G Uniform or arithmetic gradient amount, a constant increase in funds flow at the end of each period, $

GENERAL NOTATION OF COMPOUND INTEREST FACTORS

Compound interest factors were developed to facilitate economic analysis before the advent of the programmable calculator and personal computer. Today, many engineering economic evaluations are performed using spreadsheet at great ease. However, the ability to use compound interest factors will demonstrate the true skill of performing basic economic analysis. The compound interest factor follows a general format:

$(X/Y, i, n)$

In this notation, X and Y denote two sums of money, and X/Y denotes the ratio of X to Y. The letters i and n denote the interest rate and the number of interest periods, respectively. When the value of Y is given, the unknown variable X is calculated from the following;

$X (X/Y, i, n) = X *$ Compound Interest Factor

For example, given the present value P, find the future value F

$F = P (F/P, i, n)$ or simplified as $F = P (F/P)$

Compound interest factor is applied to a known variable with monetary value of $1 to calculate the unknown variable.

TABLE F.1 2% Interest Rate

n	F/P	P/F	A/F	A/P	F/A	P/A	A/G	P/G
1	1.0200	0.9804	1.0000	1.0200	1.0000	0.9804	0.0000	0.0000
2	1.0404	0.9612	0.4950	0.5150	2.0200	1.9416	0.4950	0.9612
3	1.0612	0.9423	0.3268	0.3468	3.0604	2.8839	0.9868	2.8458
4	1.0824	0.9238	0.2426	0.2626	4.1216	3.8077	1.4752	5.6173
5	1.1041	0.9057	0.1922	0.2122	5.2040	4.7135	1.9604	9.2403
6	1.1262	0.8880	0.1585	0.1785	6.3081	5.6014	2.4423	13.6801
7	1.1487	0.8706	0.1345	0.1545	7.4343	6.4720	2.9208	18.9035
8	1.1717	0.8535	0.1165	0.1365	8.5830	7.3255	3.3961	24.8779
9	1.1951	0.8368	0.1025	0.1225	9.7546	8.1622	3.8681	31.5720
10	1.2190	0.8203	0.0913	0.1113	10.9497	8.9826	4.3367	38.9551
11	1.2434	0.8043	0.0822	0.1022	12.1687	9.7868	4.8021	46.9977
12	1.2682	0.7885	0.0746	0.0946	13.4121	10.5753	5.2642	55.6712
13	1.2936	0.7730	0.0681	0.0881	14.6803	11.3484	5.7231	64.9475
14	1.3195	0.7579	0.0626	0.0826	15.9739	12.1062	6.1786	74.7999
15	1.3459	0.7430	0.0578	0.0778	17.2934	12.8493	6.6309	85.2021
16	1.3728	0.7284	0.0537	0.0737	18.6393	13.5777	7.0799	96.1288
17	1.4002	0.7142	0.0500	0.0700	20.0121	14.2919	7.5256	107.5554
18	1.4282	0.7002	0.0467	0.0667	21.4123	14.9920	7.9681	119.4581
19	1.4568	0.6864	0.0438	0.0638	22.8406	15.6785	8.4073	131.8139
20	1.4859	0.6730	0.0412	0.0612	24.2974	16.3514	8.8433	144.6003
21	1.5157	0.6598	0.0388	0.0588	25.7833	17.0112	9.2760	157.7959
22	1.5460	0.6468	0.0366	0.0566	27.2990	17.6580	9.7055	171.3795
23	1.5769	0.6342	0.0347	0.0547	28.8450	18.2922	10.1317	185.3309
24	1.6084	0.6217	0.0329	0.0529	30.4219	18.9139	10.5547	199.6305
25	1.6406	0.6095	0.0312	0.0512	32.0303	19.5235	10.9745	214.2592
26	1.6734	0.5976	0.0297	0.0497	33.6709	20.1210	11.3910	229.1987
27	1.7069	0.5859	0.0283	0.0483	35.3443	20.7069	11.8043	244.4311
28	1.7410	0.5744	0.0270	0.0470	37.0512	21.2813	12.2145	259.9392
29	1.7758	0.5631	0.0258	0.0458	38.7922	21.8444	12.6214	275.7064
30	1.8114	0.5521	0.0246	0.0446	40.5681	22.3965	13.0251	291.7164
31	1.8476	0.5412	0.0236	0.0436	42.3794	22.9377	13.4257	307.9538
32	1.8845	0.5306	0.0226	0.0426	44.2270	23.4683	13.8230	324.4035
33	1.9222	0.5202	0.0217	0.0417	46.1116	23.9886	14.2172	341.0508
34	1.9607	0.5100	0.0208	0.0408	48.0338	24.4986	14.6083	357.8817
35	1.9999	0.5000	0.0200	0.0400	49.9945	24.9986	14.9961	374.8826
36	2.0399	0.4902	0.0192	0.0392	51.9944	25.4888	15.3809	392.0405
37	2.0807	0.4806	0.0185	0.0385	54.0343	25.9695	15.7625	409.3424
38	2.1223	0.4712	0.0178	0.0378	56.1149	26.4406	16.1409	426.7764
39	2.1647	0.4619	0.0172	0.0372	58.2372	26.9026	16.5163	444.3304
40	2.2080	0.4529	0.0166	0.0366	60.4020	27.3555	16.8885	461.9931

TABLE F.2   5% Interest Rate

n	F/P	P/F	A/F	A/P	F/A	P/A	A/G	P/G
1	1.0500	0.9524	1.0000	1.0500	1.0000	0.9524	0.0000	0.0000
2	1.1025	0.9070	0.4878	0.5378	2.0500	1.8594	0.4878	0.9070
3	1.1576	0.8638	0.3172	0.3672	3.1525	2.7232	0.9675	2.6347
4	1.2155	0.8227	0.2320	0.2820	4.3101	3.5460	1.4391	5.1028
5	1.2763	0.7835	0.1810	0.2310	5.5256	4.3295	1.9025	8.2369
6	1.3401	0.7462	0.1470	0.1970	6.8019	5.0757	2.3579	11.9680
7	1.4071	0.7107	0.1228	0.1728	8.1420	5.7864	2.8052	16.2321
8	1.4775	0.6768	0.1047	0.1547	9.5491	6.4632	3.2445	20.9700
9	1.5513	0.6446	0.0907	0.1407	11.0266	7.1078	3.6758	26.1268
10	1.6289	0.6139	0.0795	0.1295	12.5779	7.7217	4.0991	31.6520
11	1.7103	0.5847	0.0704	0.1204	14.2068	8.3064	4.5144	37.4988
12	1.7959	0.5568	0.0628	0.1128	15.9171	8.8633	4.9219	43.6241
13	1.8856	0.5303	0.0565	0.1065	17.7130	9.3936	5.3215	49.9879
14	1.9799	0.5051	0.0510	0.1010	19.5986	9.8986	5.7133	56.5538
15	2.0789	0.4810	0.0463	0.0963	21.5786	10.3797	6.0973	63.2880
16	2.1829	0.4581	0.0423	0.0923	23.6575	10.8378	6.4736	70.1597
17	2.2920	0.4363	0.0387	0.0887	25.8404	11.2741	6.8423	77.1405
18	2.4066	0.4155	0.0355	0.0855	28.1324	11.6896	7.2034	84.2043
19	2.5270	0.3957	0.0327	0.0827	30.5390	12.0853	7.5569	91.3275
20	2.6533	0.3769	0.0302	0.0802	33.0660	12.4622	7.9030	98.4884
21	2.7860	0.3589	0.0280	0.0780	35.7193	12.8212	8.2416	105.6673
22	2.9253	0.3418	0.0260	0.0760	38.5052	13.1630	8.5730	112.8461
23	3.0715	0.3256	0.0241	0.0741	41.4305	13.4886	8.8971	120.0087
24	3.2251	0.3101	0.0225	0.0725	44.5020	13.7986	9.2140	127.1402
25	3.3864	0.2953	0.0210	0.0710	47.7271	14.0939	9.5238	134.2275
26	3.5557	0.2812	0.0196	0.0696	51.1135	14.3752	9.8266	141.2585
27	3.7335	0.2678	0.0183	0.0683	54.6691	14.6430	10.1224	148.2226
28	3.9201	0.2551	0.0171	0.0671	58.4026	14.8981	10.4114	155.1101
29	4.1161	0.2429	0.0160	0.0660	62.3227	15.1411	10.6936	161.9126
30	4.3219	0.2314	0.0151	0.0651	66.4388	15.3725	10.9691	168.6226
31	4.5380	0.2204	0.0141	0.0641	70.7608	15.5928	11.2381	175.2333
32	4.7649	0.2099	0.0133	0.0633	75.2988	15.8027	11.5005	181.7392
33	5.0032	0.1999	0.0125	0.0625	80.0638	16.0025	11.7566	188.1351
34	5.2533	0.1904	0.0118	0.0618	85.0670	16.1929	12.0063	194.4168
35	5.5160	0.1813	0.0111	0.0611	90.3203	16.3742	12.2498	200.5807
36	5.7918	0.1727	0.0104	0.0604	95.8363	16.5469	12.4872	206.6237
37	6.0814	0.1644	0.0098	0.0598	101.6281	16.7113	12.7186	212.5434
38	6.3855	0.1566	0.0093	0.0593	107.7095	16.8679	12.9440	218.3378
39	6.7048	0.1491	0.0088	0.0588	114.0950	17.0170	13.1636	224.0054
40	7.0400	0.1420	0.0083	0.0583	120.7998	17.1591	13.3775	229.5452

TABLE F.3 6% Interest Rate

n	F/P	P/F	A/F	A/P	F/A	P/A	A/G	P/G
1	1.0600	0.9434	1.0000	1.0600	1.0000	0.9434	0.0000	0.0000
2	1.1236	0.8900	0.4854	0.5454	2.0600	1.8334	0.4854	0.8900
3	1.1910	0.8396	0.3141	0.3741	3.1836	2.6730	0.9612	2.5692
4	1.2625	0.7921	0.2286	0.2886	4.3746	3.4651	1.4272	4.9455
5	1.3382	0.7473	0.1774	0.2374	5.6371	4.2124	1.8836	7.9345
6	1.4185	0.7050	0.1434	0.2034	6.9753	4.9173	2.3304	11.4594
7	1.5036	0.6651	0.1191	0.1791	8.3938	5.5824	2.7676	15.4497
8	1.5938	0.6274	0.1010	0.1610	9.8975	6.2098	3.1952	19.8416
9	1.6895	0.5919	0.0870	0.1470	11.4913	6.8017	3.6133	24.5768
10	1.7908	0.5584	0.0759	0.1359	13.1808	7.3601	4.0220	29.6023
11	1.8983	0.5268	0.0668	0.1268	14.9716	7.8869	4.4213	34.8702
12	2.0122	0.4970	0.0593	0.1193	16.8699	8.3838	4.8113	40.3369
13	2.1329	0.4688	0.0530	0.1130	18.8821	8.8527	5.1920	45.9629
14	2.2609	0.4423	0.0476	0.1076	21.0151	9.2950	5.5635	51.7128
15	2.3966	0.4173	0.0430	0.1030	23.2760	9.7122	5.9260	57.5546
16	2.5404	0.3936	0.0390	0.0990	25.6725	10.1059	6.2794	63.4592
17	2.6928	0.3714	0.0354	0.0954	28.2129	10.4773	6.6240	69.4011
18	2.8543	0.3503	0.0324	0.0924	30.9057	10.8276	6.9597	75.3569
19	3.0256	0.3305	0.0296	0.0896	33.7600	11.1581	7.2867	81.3062
20	3.2071	0.3118	0.0272	0.0872	36.7856	11.4699	7.6051	87.2304
21	3.3996	0.2942	0.0250	0.0850	39.9927	11.7641	7.9151	93.1136
22	3.6035	0.2775	0.0230	0.0830	43.3923	12.0416	8.2166	98.9412
23	3.8197	0.2618	0.0213	0.0813	46.9958	12.3034	8.5099	104.7007
24	4.0489	0.2470	0.0197	0.0797	50.8156	12.5504	8.7951	110.3812
25	4.2919	0.2330	0.0182	0.0782	54.8645	12.7834	9.0722	115.9732
26	4.5494	0.2198	0.0169	0.0769	59.1564	13.0032	9.3414	121.4684
27	4.8223	0.2074	0.0157	0.0757	63.7058	13.2105	9.6029	126.8600
28	5.1117	0.1956	0.0146	0.0746	68.5281	13.4062	9.8568	132.1420
29	5.4184	0.1846	0.0136	0.0736	73.6398	13.5907	10.1032	137.3096
30	5.7435	0.1741	0.0126	0.0726	79.0582	13.7648	10.3422	142.3588
31	6.0881	0.1643	0.0118	0.0718	84.8017	13.9291	10.5740	147.2864
32	6.4534	0.1550	0.0110	0.0710	90.8898	14.0840	10.7988	152.0901
33	6.8406	0.1462	0.0103	0.0703	97.3432	14.2302	11.0166	156.7681
34	7.2510	0.1379	0.0096	0.0696	104.1838	14.3681	11.2276	161.3192
35	7.6861	0.1301	0.0090	0.0690	111.4348	14.4982	11.4319	165.7427
36	8.1473	0.1227	0.0084	0.0684	119.1209	14.6210	11.6298	170.0387
37	8.6361	0.1158	0.0079	0.0679	127.2681	14.7368	11.8213	174.2072
38	9.1543	0.1092	0.0074	0.0674	135.9042	14.8460	12.0065	178.2490
39	9.7035	0.1031	0.0069	0.0669	145.0585	14.9491	12.1857	182.1652
40	10.2857	0.0972	0.0065	0.0665	154.7620	15.0463	12.3590	185.9568

TABLE F.4   8% Interest Rate

n	F/P	P/F	A/F	A/P	F/A	P/A	A/G	P/G
1	1.0800	0.9259	1.0000	1.0800	1.0000	0.9259	0.0000	0.0000
2	1.1664	0.8573	0.4808	0.5608	2.0800	1.7833	0.4808	0.8573
3	1.2597	0.7938	0.3080	0.3880	3.2464	2.5771	0.9487	2.4450
4	1.3605	0.7350	0.2219	0.3019	4.5061	3.3121	1.4040	4.6501
5	1.4693	0.6806	0.1705	0.2505	5.8666	3.9927	1.8465	7.3724
6	1.5869	0.6302	0.1363	0.2163	7.3359	4.6229	2.2763	10.5233
7	1.7138	0.5835	0.1121	0.1921	8.9228	5.2064	2.6937	14.0242
8	1.8509	0.5403	0.0940	0.1740	10.6366	5.7466	3.0985	17.8061
9	1.9990	0.5002	0.0801	0.1601	12.4876	6.2469	3.4910	21.8081
10	2.1589	0.4632	0.0690	0.1490	14.4866	6.7101	3.8713	25.9768
11	2.3316	0.4289	0.0601	0.1401	16.6455	7.1390	4.2395	30.2657
12	2.5182	0.3971	0.0527	0.1327	18.9771	7.5361	4.5957	34.6339
13	2.7196	0.3677	0.0465	0.1265	21.4953	7.9038	4.9402	39.0463
14	2.9372	0.3405	0.0413	0.1213	24.2149	8.2442	5.2731	43.4723
15	3.1722	0.3152	0.0368	0.1168	27.1521	8.5595	5.5945	47.8857
16	3.4259	0.2919	0.0330	0.1130	30.3243	8.8514	5.9046	52.2640
17	3.7000	0.2703	0.0296	0.1096	33.7502	9.1216	6.2037	56.5883
18	3.9960	0.2502	0.0267	0.1067	37.4502	9.3719	6.4920	60.8426
19	4.3157	0.2317	0.0241	0.1041	41.4463	9.6036	6.7697	65.0134
20	4.6610	0.2145	0.0219	0.1019	45.7620	9.8181	7.0369	69.0898
21	5.0338	0.1987	0.0198	0.0998	50.4229	10.0168	7.2940	73.0629
22	5.4365	0.1839	0.0180	0.0980	55.4568	10.2007	7.5412	76.9257
23	5.8715	0.1703	0.0164	0.0964	60.8933	10.3711	7.7786	80.6726
24	6.3412	0.1577	0.0150	0.0950	66.7648	10.5288	8.0066	84.2997
25	6.8485	0.1460	0.0137	0.0937	73.1059	10.6748	8.2254	87.8041
26	7.3964	0.1352	0.0125	0.0925	79.9544	10.8100	8.4352	91.1842
27	7.9881	0.1252	0.0114	0.0914	87.3508	10.9352	8.6363	94.4390
28	8.6271	0.1159	0.0105	0.0905	95.3388	11.0511	8.8289	97.5687
29	9.3173	0.1073	0.0096	0.0896	103.9659	11.1584	9.0133	100.5738
30	10.0627	0.0994	0.0088	0.0888	113.2832	11.2578	9.1897	103.4558
31	10.8677	0.0920	0.0081	0.0881	123.3459	11.3498	9.3584	106.2163
32	11.7371	0.0852	0.0075	0.0875	134.2135	11.4350	9.5197	108.8575
33	12.6760	0.0789	0.0069	0.0869	145.9506	11.5139	9.6737	111.3819
34	13.6901	0.0730	0.0063	0.0863	158.6267	11.5869	9.8208	113.7924
35	14.7853	0.0676	0.0058	0.0858	172.3168	11.6546	9.9611	116.0920
36	15.9682	0.0626	0.0053	0.0853	187.1021	11.7172	10.0949	118.2839
37	17.2456	0.0580	0.0049	0.0849	203.0703	11.7752	10.2225	120.3713
38	18.6253	0.0537	0.0045	0.0845	220.3159	11.8289	10.3440	122.3579
39	20.1153	0.0497	0.0042	0.0842	238.9412	11.8786	10.4597	124.2470
40	21.7245	0.0460	0.0039	0.0839	259.0565	11.9246	10.5699	126.0422

TABLE F.5 10% Interest Rate

n	F/P	P/F	A/F	A/P	F/A	P/A	A/G	P/G
1	1.1000	0.9091	1.0000	1.1000	1.0000	0.9091	0.0000	0.0000
2	1.2100	0.8264	0.4762	0.5762	2.1000	1.7355	0.4762	0.8264
3	1.3310	0.7513	0.3021	0.4021	3.3100	2.4869	0.9366	2.3291
4	1.4641	0.6830	0.2155	0.3155	4.6410	3.1699	1.3812	4.3781
5	1.6105	0.6209	0.1638	0.2638	6.1051	3.7908	1.8101	6.8618
6	1.7716	0.5645	0.1296	0.2296	7.7156	4.3553	2.2236	9.6842
7	1.9487	0.5132	0.1054	0.2054	9.4872	4.8684	2.6216	12.7631
8	2.1436	0.4665	0.0874	0.1874	11.4359	5.3349	3.0045	16.0287
9	2.3579	0.4241	0.0736	0.1736	13.5795	5.7590	3.3724	19.4215
10	2.5937	0.3855	0.0627	0.1627	15.9374	6.1446	3.7255	22.8913
11	2.8531	0.3505	0.0540	0.1540	18.5312	6.4951	4.0641	26.3963
12	3.1384	0.3186	0.0468	0.1468	21.3843	6.8137	4.3884	29.9012
13	3.4523	0.2897	0.0408	0.1408	24.5227	7.1034	4.6988	33.3772
14	3.7975	0.2633	0.0357	0.1357	27.9750	7.3667	4.9955	36.8005
15	4.1772	0.2394	0.0315	0.1315	31.7725	7.6061	5.2789	40.1520
16	4.5950	0.2176	0.0278	0.1278	35.9497	7.8237	5.5493	43.4164
17	5.0545	0.1978	0.0247	0.1247	40.5447	8.0216	5.8071	46.5819
18	5.5599	0.1799	0.0219	0.1219	45.5992	8.2014	6.0526	49.6395
19	6.1159	0.1635	0.0195	0.1195	51.1591	8.3649	6.2861	52.5827
20	6.7275	0.1486	0.0175	0.1175	57.2750	8.5136	6.5081	55.4069
21	7.4002	0.1351	0.0156	0.1156	64.0025	8.6487	6.7189	58.1095
22	8.1403	0.1228	0.0140	0.1140	71.4027	8.7715	6.9189	60.6893
23	8.9543	0.1117	0.0126	0.1126	79.5430	8.8832	7.1085	63.1462
24	9.8497	0.1015	0.0113	0.1113	88.4973	8.9847	7.2881	65.4813
25	10.8347	0.0923	0.0102	0.1102	98.3471	9.0770	7.4580	67.6964
26	11.9182	0.0839	0.0092	0.1092	109.1818	9.1609	7.6186	69.7940
27	13.1100	0.0763	0.0083	0.1083	121.0999	9.2372	7.7704	71.7773
28	14.4210	0.0693	0.0075	0.1075	134.2099	9.3066	7.9137	73.6495
29	15.8631	0.0630	0.0067	0.1067	148.6309	9.3696	8.0489	75.4146
30	17.4494	0.0573	0.0061	0.1061	164.4940	9.4269	8.1762	77.0766
31	19.1943	0.0521	0.0055	0.1055	181.9434	9.4790	8.2962	78.6395
32	21.1138	0.0474	0.0050	0.1050	201.1378	9.5264	8.4091	80.1078
33	23.2252	0.0431	0.0045	0.1045	222.2515	9.5694	8.5152	81.4856
34	25.5477	0.0391	0.0041	0.1041	245.4767	9.6086	8.6149	82.7773
35	28.1024	0.0356	0.0037	0.1037	271.0244	9.6442	8.7086	83.9872
36	30.9127	0.0323	0.0033	0.1033	299.1268	9.6765	8.7965	85.1194
37	34.0039	0.0294	0.0030	0.1030	330.0395	9.7059	8.8789	86.1781
38	37.4043	0.0267	0.0027	0.1027	364.0434	9.7327	8.9562	87.1673
39	41.1448	0.0243	0.0025	0.1025	401.4478	9.7570	9.0285	88.0908
40	45.2593	0.0221	0.0023	0.1023	442.5926	9.7791	9.0962	88.9525

TABLE F.6   12% Interest Rate

n	F/P	P/F	A/F	A/P	F/A	P/A	A/G	P/G
1	1.1200	0.8929	1.0000	1.1200	1.0000	0.8929	0.0000	0.0000
2	1.2544	0.7972	0.4717	0.5917	2.1200	1.6901	0.4717	0.7972
3	1.4049	0.7118	0.2963	0.4163	3.3744	2.4018	0.9246	2.2208
4	1.5735	0.6355	0.2092	0.3292	4.7793	3.0373	1.3589	4.1273
5	1.7623	0.5674	0.1574	0.2774	6.3528	3.6048	1.7746	6.3970
6	1.9738	0.5066	0.1232	0.2432	8.1152	4.1114	2.1720	8.9302
7	2.2107	0.4523	0.0991	0.2191	10.0890	4.5638	2.5515	11.6443
8	2.4760	0.4039	0.0813	0.2013	12.2997	4.9676	2.9131	14.4714
9	2.7731	0.3606	0.0677	0.1877	14.7757	5.3282	3.2574	17.3563
10	3.1058	0.3220	0.0570	0.1770	17.5487	5.6502	3.5847	20.2541
11	3.4785	0.2875	0.0484	0.1684	20.6546	5.9377	3.8953	23.1288
12	3.8960	0.2567	0.0414	0.1614	24.1331	6.1944	4.1897	25.9523
13	4.3635	0.2292	0.0357	0.1557	28.0291	6.4235	4.4683	28.7024
14	4.8871	0.2046	0.0309	0.1509	32.3926	6.6282	4.7317	31.3624
15	5.4736	0.1827	0.0268	0.1468	37.2797	6.8109	4.9803	33.9202
16	6.1304	0.1631	0.0234	0.1434	42.7533	6.9740	5.2147	36.3670
17	6.8660	0.1456	0.0205	0.1405	48.8837	7.1196	5.4353	38.6973
18	7.6900	0.1300	0.0179	0.1379	55.7497	7.2497	5.6427	40.9080
19	8.6128	0.1161	0.0158	0.1358	63.4397	7.3658	5.8375	42.9979
20	9.6463	0.1037	0.0139	0.1339	72.0524	7.4694	6.0202	44.9676
21	10.8038	0.0926	0.0122	0.1322	81.6987	7.5620	6.1913	46.8188
22	12.1003	0.0826	0.0108	0.1308	92.5026	7.6446	6.3514	48.5543
23	13.5523	0.0738	0.0096	0.1296	104.6029	7.7184	6.5010	50.1776
24	15.1786	0.0659	0.0085	0.1285	118.1552	7.7843	6.6406	51.6929
25	17.0001	0.0588	0.0075	0.1275	133.3339	7.8431	6.7708	53.1046
26	19.0401	0.0525	0.0067	0.1267	150.3339	7.8957	6.8921	54.4177
27	21.3249	0.0469	0.0059	0.1259	169.3740	7.9426	7.0049	55.6369
28	23.8839	0.0419	0.0052	0.1252	190.6989	7.9844	7.1098	56.7674
29	26.7499	0.0374	0.0047	0.1247	214.5828	8.0218	7.2071	57.8141
30	29.9599	0.0334	0.0041	0.1241	241.3327	8.0552	7.2974	58.7821
31	33.5551	0.0298	0.0037	0.1237	271.2926	8.0850	7.3811	59.6761
32	37.5817	0.0266	0.0033	0.1233	304.8477	8.1116	7.4586	60.5010
33	42.0915	0.0238	0.0029	0.1229	342.4294	8.1354	7.5302	61.2612
34	47.1425	0.0212	0.0026	0.1226	384.5210	8.1566	7.5965	61.9612
35	52.7996	0.0189	0.0023	0.1223	431.6635	8.1755	7.6577	62.6052
36	59.1356	0.0169	0.0021	0.1221	484.4631	8.1924	7.7141	63.1970
37	66.2318	0.0151	0.0018	0.1218	543.5987	8.2075	7.7661	63.7406
38	74.1797	0.0135	0.0016	0.1216	609.8305	8.2210	7.8141	64.2394
39	83.0812	0.0120	0.0015	0.1215	684.0102	8.2330	7.8582	64.6967
40	93.0510	0.0107	0.0013	0.1213	767.0914	8.2438	7.8988	65.1159

TABLE F.7   15% Interest Rate

n	F/P	P/F	A/F	A/P	F/A	P/A	A/G	P/G
1	1.1500	0.8696	1.0000	1.1500	1.0000	0.8696	0.0000	0.0000
2	1.3225	0.7561	0.4651	0.6151	2.1500	1.6257	0.4651	0.7561
3	1.5209	0.6575	0.2880	0.4380	3.4725	2.2832	0.9071	2.0712
4	1.7490	0.5718	0.2003	0.3503	4.9934	2.8550	1.3263	3.7864
5	2.0114	0.4972	0.1483	0.2983	6.7424	3.3522	1.7228	5.7751
6	2.3131	0.4323	0.1142	0.2642	8.7537	3.7845	2.0972	7.9368
7	2.6600	0.3759	0.0904	0.2404	11.0668	4.1604	2.4498	10.1924
8	3.0590	0.3269	0.0729	0.2229	13.7268	4.4873	2.7813	12.4807
9	3.5179	0.2843	0.0596	0.2096	16.7858	4.7716	3.0922	14.7548
10	4.0456	0.2472	0.0493	0.1993	20.3037	5.0188	3.3832	16.9795
11	4.6524	0.2149	0.0411	0.1911	24.3493	5.2337	3.6549	19.1289
12	5.3503	0.1869	0.0345	0.1845	29.0017	5.4206	3.9082	21.1849
13	6.1528	0.1625	0.0291	0.1791	34.3519	5.5831	4.1438	23.1352
14	7.0757	0.1413	0.0247	0.1747	40.5047	5.7245	4.3624	24.9725
15	8.1371	0.1229	0.0210	0.1710	47.5804	5.8474	4.5650	26.6930
16	9.3576	0.1069	0.0179	0.1679	55.7175	5.9542	4.7522	28.2960
17	10.7613	0.0929	0.0154	0.1654	65.0751	6.0472	4.9251	29.7828
18	12.3755	0.0808	0.0132	0.1632	75.8364	6.1280	5.0843	31.1565
19	14.2318	0.0703	0.0113	0.1613	88.2118	6.1982	5.2307	32.4213
20	16.3665	0.0611	0.0098	0.1598	102.4436	6.2593	5.3651	33.5822
21	18.8215	0.0531	0.0084	0.1584	118.8101	6.3125	5.4883	34.6448
22	21.6447	0.0462	0.0073	0.1573	137.6316	6.3587	5.6010	35.6150
23	24.8915	0.0402	0.0063	0.1563	159.2764	6.3988	5.7040	36.4988
24	28.6252	0.0349	0.0054	0.1554	184.1678	6.4338	5.7979	37.3023
25	32.9190	0.0304	0.0047	0.1547	212.7930	6.4641	5.8834	38.0314
26	37.8568	0.0264	0.0041	0.1541	245.7120	6.4906	5.9612	38.6918
27	43.5353	0.0230	0.0035	0.1535	283.5688	6.5135	6.0319	39.2890
28	50.0656	0.0200	0.0031	0.1531	327.1041	6.5335	6.0960	39.8283
29	57.5755	0.0174	0.0027	0.1527	377.1697	6.5509	6.1541	40.3146
30	66.2118	0.0151	0.0023	0.1523	434.7451	6.5660	6.2066	40.7526
31	76.1435	0.0131	0.0020	0.1520	500.9569	6.5791	6.2541	41.1466
32	87.5651	0.0114	0.0017	0.1517	577.1005	6.5905	6.2970	41.5006
33	100.6998	0.0099	0.0015	0.1515	664.6655	6.6005	6.3357	41.8184
34	115.8048	0.0086	0.0013	0.1513	765.3654	6.6091	6.3705	42.1033
35	133.1755	0.0075	0.0011	0.1511	881.1702	6.6166	6.4019	42.3586
36	153.1519	0.0065	0.0010	0.1510	1014.3457	6.6231	6.4301	42.5872
37	176.1246	0.0057	0.0009	0.1509	1167.4975	6.6288	6.4554	42.7916
38	202.5433	0.0049	0.0007	0.1507	1343.6222	6.6338	6.4781	42.9743
39	232.9248	0.0043	0.0006	0.1506	1546.1655	6.6380	6.4985	43.1374
40	267.8635	0.0037	0.0006	0.1506	1779.0903	6.6418	6.5168	43.2830

TABLE F.8 20% Interest Rate

n	F/P	P/F	A/F	A/P	F/A	P/A	A/G	P/G
1	1.2000	0.8333	1.0000	1.2000	1.0000	0.8333	0.0000	0.0000
2	1.4400	0.6944	0.4545	0.6545	2.2000	1.5278	0.4545	0.6944
3	1.7280	0.5787	0.2747	0.4747	3.6400	2.1065	0.8791	1.8519
4	2.0736	0.4823	0.1863	0.3863	5.3680	2.5887	1.2742	3.2986
5	2.4883	0.4019	0.1344	0.3344	7.4416	2.9906	1.6405	4.9061
6	2.9860	0.3349	0.1007	0.3007	9.9299	3.3255	1.9788	6.5806
7	3.5832	0.2791	0.0774	0.2774	12.9159	3.6046	2.2902	8.2551
8	4.2998	0.2326	0.0606	0.2606	16.4991	3.8372	2.5756	9.8831
9	5.1598	0.1938	0.0481	0.2481	20.7989	4.0310	2.8364	11.4335
10	6.1917	0.1615	0.0385	0.2385	25.9587	4.1925	3.0739	12.8871
11	7.4301	0.1346	0.0311	0.2311	32.1504	4.3271	3.2893	14.2330
12	8.9161	0.1122	0.0253	0.2253	39.5805	4.4392	3.4841	15.4667
13	10.6993	0.0935	0.0206	0.2206	48.4966	4.5327	3.6597	16.5883
14	12.8392	0.0779	0.0169	0.2169	59.1959	4.6106	3.8175	17.6008
15	15.4070	0.0649	0.0139	0.2139	72.0351	4.6755	3.9588	18.5095
16	18.4884	0.0541	0.0114	0.2114	87.4421	4.7296	4.0851	19.3208
17	22.1861	0.0451	0.0094	0.2094	105.9306	4.7746	4.1976	20.0419
18	26.6233	0.0376	0.0078	0.2078	128.1167	4.8122	4.2975	20.6805
19	31.9480	0.0313	0.0065	0.2065	154.7400	4.8435	4.3861	21.2439
20	38.3376	0.0261	0.0054	0.2054	186.6880	4.8696	4.4643	21.7395
21	46.0051	0.0217	0.0044	0.2044	225.0256	4.8913	4.5334	22.1742
22	55.2061	0.0181	0.0037	0.2037	271.0307	4.9094	4.5941	22.5546
23	66.2474	0.0151	0.0031	0.2031	326.2369	4.9245	4.6475	22.8867
24	79.4968	0.0126	0.0025	0.2025	392.4842	4.9371	4.6943	23.1760
25	95.3962	0.0105	0.0021	0.2021	471.9811	4.9476	4.7352	23.4276
26	114.4755	0.0087	0.0018	0.2018	567.3773	4.9563	4.7709	23.6460
27	137.3706	0.0073	0.0015	0.2015	681.8528	4.9636	4.8020	23.8353
28	164.8447	0.0061	0.0012	0.2012	819.2233	4.9697	4.8291	23.9991
29	197.8136	0.0051	0.0010	0.2010	984.0680	4.9747	4.8527	24.1406
30	237.3763	0.0042	0.0008	0.2008	1181.8816	4.9789	4.8731	24.2628
31	284.8516	0.0035	0.0007	0.2007	1419.2579	4.9824	4.8908	24.3681
32	341.8219	0.0029	0.0006	0.2006	1704.1095	4.9854	4.9061	24.4588
33	410.1863	0.0024	0.0005	0.2005	2045.9314	4.9878	4.9194	24.5368
34	492.2235	0.0020	0.0004	0.2004	2456.1176	4.9898	4.9308	24.6038
35	590.6682	0.0017	0.0003	0.2003	2948.3411	4.9915	4.9406	24.6614
36	708.8019	0.0014	0.0003	0.2003	3539.0094	4.9929	4.9491	24.7108
37	850.5622	0.0012	0.0002	0.2002	4247.8112	4.9941	4.9564	24.7531
38	1020.6747	0.0010	0.0002	0.2002	5098.3735	4.9951	4.9627	24.7894
39	1224.8096	0.0008	0.0002	0.2002	6119.0482	4.9959	4.9681	24.8204
40	1469.7716	0.0007	0.0001	0.2001	7343.8578	4.9966	4.9728	24.8469

Made in the USA
Las Vegas, NV
05 December 2023

82135613R00176